My Soul Magnifies the Lord

A Scriptural Journey with Mary

Jeanne Kun

the WORD among us

Handwritten annotations:

Studio 2000
733-1906 L.M.

Plenary Indulgence — Baltimore Cathechism

God made me
to know him,
to love him +
to serve him with
to be happy with
to him in Heaven.

Prayers

— Memorare
— St. Michael Prayer

Vickie
pg. 1199

— Life - New Revolution
— Consecration to Mary
— Imitation of Christ

Pizza
Taco in bag

Book:
"Left to Tell"
— Denis - Janis
Brian ⑦

Advent ⑥
Katesy - Boundaries ⑤
Call Natalie

Maura Lafaro - 8537 L.M.
④ Nat. Fam. Plan.

③ Deacon Doug - Dauna
Code
L.M. 734-7787

② Adoration

Nov. 5 ①
Teresa Donnely - Guidke
733-1906

The Word Among Us
9639 Doctor Perry Road
Ijamsville, Maryland 21754
www.wordamongus.org

Poems *Advent Overture, Visitation Day, The Road to Bethlehem, Anna's Heir, Journey by Starlight, Freed from the Fowler's Snare, In Mary's Steps, Mary's Bidding, Pietà,* and *Pentecost Vigil,* copyright © 2003 by Jeanne Kun. All rights reserved. Used by permission.

Cover and Book Design: David Crosson

Scripture passages contained herein are from the Revised Standard Version Bible: Catholic Edition, © 1965 and 1966 by the Division of Christian Education of the National Council of the Churches of Christ in the U.S.A. All rights reserved. Used by permission.

Cover image: Gerard David, *The Rest on the Flight into Egypt,* c. 1510
© 2003 Board of Trustees, National Gallery of Art, Washington, D.C.

Nihil obstat: Reverend Monsignor Vincent J. Haut, VG
               Censor Librorum
               July 22, 2003

Imprimatur: +Most Reverend Victor Galeone
               Bishop of Saint Augustine
               July 25, 2003

ISBN: 1-59325-023-1

Library of Congress Control Number: 2003111631

Made and printed in the United States of America.

Contents

Introduction   *4*

Reflection 1:
The Annunciation   *8*

Reflection 2:
The Visitation   *24*

Reflection 3:
The Nativity   *40*

Reflection 4:
The Presentation   *58*

Reflection 5:
The Adoration of the Magi   *74*

Reflection 6:
The Flight into Egypt   *92*

Reflection 7:
The Finding of the Child Jesus in the Temple   *110*

Reflection 8:
The Wedding at Cana   *126*

Reflection 9:
At the Foot of the Cross   *142*

Reflection 10:
Pentecost   *158*

Source Notes and Acknowledgments   *175*

Introduction

"Live as the Blessed Virgin lived: loving God only, desiring God only, trying to please God only in all that we do." This was the wise advice given by St. John Vianney to his parishioners in the French village of Ars more than a century ago, and it is still applicable for us today. *My Soul Magnifies the Lord: A Scriptural Journey with Mary* provides readers with the opportunity to examine the life of the Blessed Virgin Mary and come to know her in a deeper way. As we accompany Mary on her pilgrimage of faith, we learn about the woman who magnified the Lord in such a profound way. And from Mary, who bore the Word made flesh, we learn how to follow her son, Jesus.

Since God chose this young Jewish woman to enter into his work of redemption, we are often tempted to think of Mary as so perfect that she is beyond emulation. We may envision her as a beautifully crafted statue atop a tall pedestal or a stately queen enthroned in the heights of heaven. Yet, while Mary was privileged to be chosen by God and filled with grace to prepare her for her unique role, she was nonetheless an ordinary young woman of Israel.

Perhaps barely more than a girl when the angel Gabriel brought God's bewildering request to her, Mary must have been greatly challenged to believe God and the mysteries he was asking her to participate in. Without hesitation, however, she gave her assent. As the mother of Jesus, the Incarnate Son of God,

Mary caught him in her arms when he took his first faltering steps, witnessed his first miracle at Cana, and wept as he died on the cross.

The New Testament does not provide a physical description of Mary (nor, for that matter, of Jesus). In all likelihood, she had the distinguishing features and other physical traits—complexion and color of hair—of any woman of her times of Semitic descent, but we know no more about her appearance than we know about her son's. Surely, though, there was a close family resemblance between them, since Mary was Jesus' biological mother.

The Gospels are also silent about Mary's birth and death. None of the evangelists wrote a biography of Mary, and none gave us the kind of vital statistics and curriculum vitae that would be found in the latest edition of *Who's Who*. We will be disappointed if we are looking for such particulars about Mary as we read the New Testament.

However, the few scenes painted by Matthew, Mark, Luke, and John in which Mary played a role portray all that is essential in order for us to know her. These events—the "Marian moments" of the Bible—depict an accurate portrait of her heart and character and also clearly tell us who Mary is: woman of faith; Virgin Mother of the Lord; intercessor; Mother of the church.

Where did the evangelists receive the information about Mary and about Jesus' infancy? We can assume that, in the earliest days of the church, Mary "passed on to the disciples her memories of the Incarnation, the infancy, the hidden life and the mission of her divine Son as a priceless treasure, thus helping to make him known and to strengthen the faith of believers" (Pope John Paul II, General audience of May 28, 1997). In revealing her knowledge and memories about her son, Mary also revealed much about herself.

Through the centuries, tradition and the teaching authority of the Catholic Church have given us much to treasure about Mary by deepening our understanding of biblical truths. In A.D. 431, at the Council of Ephesus, the church accorded to Mary the title "Mother of God" (*Catechism of the Catholic Church*, 466). The early church also affirmed its faith in Mary's perpetual virginity (CCC, 499). The church's recognition that Mary, "full of grace," was redeemed from the moment of her conception culminated in the dogma of the Immaculate Conception, defined in 1854 (CCC, 491). In 1950, the church defined the dogma of the Assumption of Mary. Since Mary had been preserved from sin, she was also preserved from physical decay, the punishment for sin. And so our pilgrimage with the Blessed Virgin ends in the glorious hope of our own bodily resurrection (CCC, 966).

How to Use This Book

In *My Soul Magnifies the Lord: A Scriptural Journey with Mary*, we accompany Mary through the crucial events of her life, and she accompanies us on our pilgrimage of faith. Each chapter focuses on a "scene" from her life as recorded in the New Testament. As you begin each reflection, carefully read the Scripture narrative—provided in this book in the Revised Standard Version—and meditate on it. Also read the accompanying section "Reflecting on the Word" to deepen your understanding of the text.

Two sets of questions are included in each chapter to help you explore the full scope of the passage and consider its relevance to your own life. Those under the heading "Pondering the Word" require an attentive reading of the Scripture selection and focus on the content and meaning of the text. "Living the Word" questions prompt you to apply the lessons and truths learned through Scripture to your own life.

"Rooted in the Word" offers brief comments on various attributes of Mary as well as of others in the Bible—among them Ruth, Hannah, and Abraham—that are modeled in the corresponding scene. Additional Scripture texts further illustrate the virtue or character trait highlighted in this section. A selection from a Catholic writer—ancient or modern—concludes each chapter. These excerpts, under the heading "Treasuring the Word," are indeed treasures from the church's rich Marian heritage.

The format of *My Soul Magnifies the Lord* is suited to personal reflection and individual study as well as group discussion. In either case, begin each session with prayer, asking God to speak to you through his word. Although each chapter's Scripture scene is provided in full in this book, you may find it helpful to have a Bible on hand for looking up other passages and cross-references.

Whether you use this book for personal study or as an aid in your prayer time, read at your own pace, taking the time to meditate on the material and pursue any thoughts it brings to mind. You will gain the most benefit from your study by writing your answers to the questions in the space provided. End your reading or study with a prayer of thanksgiving to God for what you have learned and ask the Holy Spirit how to apply it to your life.

If you use this book in a Bible study group, it is especially important that each member take the time to prepare well for each session. Read the material decided upon in advance and consider your answers to the questions so the group can have a rewarding discussion in the time allotted. Actively contribute to the discussion, but also listen attentively to the others in the group. Respect each member of the group and their contribution to the discussion. The group might also want to designate a leader or moderator to facilitate the discussion and to include a time of prayer together during the meeting.

As you progress through the events of Mary's life, we pray that you too will be filled with the grace that God so lavishly poured upon his mother. On that day when Mary told her cousin Elizabeth about the great miracle that had come to pass within her, she proclaimed that her soul magnified the Lord (Luke 1:46). As we grow closer to Jesus through his mother, may our own souls reflect the Lord and the glory he has in store for all of us.

Jeanne Kun
The Word Among Us

The Annunciation

Behold, I am the handmaid of the Lord; let it be to me according to your word.
Luke 1:38

Our Lady was full of God because she lived for God alone, yet she thought of herself only as the handmaid of the Lord. Let us do the same.
Blessed Mother Teresa of Calcutta, *Jesus, the Word to Be Spoken*

Advent Overture

Might Gabriel have gasped in wonder
at the task entrusted him:
To be herald
of God's generosity and deed
that would clothe all majesty in humility?

Did he quail
to bring such request from eternal divinity
to an earthly child's mortality?

Did he hesitate
at the sight of the fragile virginity before him,
fearing whether this frail womb could bear God's weight
and contain infinity within its walls?

Then resolutely
Gabriel's greeting broke upon Mary,
plowing furrows
in the fertile silence of her soul
so God's word might be planted there
like seed in a readied field.

Did the angel tremble then
while waiting this child's answer,
anxious that she not refuse?

And then she gave consent.

The seed was sown,
the Word conceived.
God found home upon the earth
and would receive a mother's warm embrace.

Perhaps Gabriel sighed in relief with task accomplished
and the angel-hosts of heaven sang their joy at her reply
(and already hide their faces in reverence at his flesh
soon to lie naked against the raw wood of the manger and the cross).

Then silence folded in again
around the virgin child
as Gabriel took leave of her.
But she was not alone,
for with her *fiat* Mary's heart
had begun to beat in unison (and full accord)
with the One now growing in her womb.

Luke 1:26-38 *The Scene*

¹:²⁶ In the sixth month the angel Gabriel was sent from God to a city of Galilee named Nazareth, ²⁷ to a virgin betrothed to a man whose name was Joseph, of the house of David; and the virgin's name was Mary. ²⁸ And he came to her and said, "Hail, full of grace, the Lord is with you!" ²⁹ But she was greatly troubled at the saying, and considered in her mind what sort of greeting this might be. ³⁰ And the angel said to her, "Do not be afraid, Mary, for you have found favor with God. ³¹And behold, you will conceive in your womb and bear a son, and you shall call his name Jesus.

³² He will be great, and will be called the
    Son of the Most High;
and the Lord God will give to him the
    throne of his father David,
³³ and he will reign over the house of
    Jacob for ever;
and of his kingdom there will be no end."

³⁴ And Mary said to the angel, "How can this be, since I have no husband?" ³⁵And the angel said to her,
    "The Holy Spirit will come upon you,
    and the power of the Most High
        will overshadow you;
    therefore the child to be born will be
        called holy,
    the Son of God.
³⁶ And behold, your kinswoman Elizabeth in her old age has also conceived a son; and this is the sixth month with her who was called barren. ³⁷ For with God nothing will be impossible." ³⁸ And Mary said, "Behold, I am the handmaid of the Lord; let it be to me according to your word." And the angel departed from her.

Reflecting on the Word

Since the beginning, God has spoken with the men and women whom he created. First, he revealed himself to Adam and Eve so that they might know him and enjoy fellowship with him—a relationship so movingly described as "God walking in the garden in the cool of the day" amid his creation (Genesis 3:8). Thus, the story of Adam and Eve's fall is a wrenching illustration of the sin that separates the human race from its creator. Yet, when our first parents were disobedient, God did not stop speaking to them, nor did he let his plan for his creation be thwarted. Even as Adam and Eve tried to excuse their fault (3:12-13), God spoke his first words of promise to reverse the consequences of sin and to triumph over Satan, giving a hint of hope of the redemption to come: Eve's offspring would crush the serpent (3:15).

After the fall, humankind began its long wait for a savior. Through the centuries, God continued his conversation with his chosen people as he spoke to the patriarchs and prophets of Israel, repeatedly renewing his promise. Finally the long-awaited time is at hand: God enters into conversation once again, this time with Mary of Nazareth. Out of this unique conversation, the Word becomes flesh.

The angel Gabriel's words to Mary, "Hail, full of grace" (Luke 1:28), announce a radical new turn in God's dialogue with humankind. God singles out a young Jewish woman and, through Gabriel, makes a mo-mentous request of her: to bear the "Son of the Most High" (1:31-32). Mary's question, "How can this be, since I have no husband?" (1:34), is not a skeptic's demand for proof that ends any further discussion; rather, with her inquiry, she enters more deeply into the conversation, expressing a willingness to grasp something holy and mysterious.

In answer, Gabriel offers Mary no physiological explanation because Jesus is to be conceived in a way that surpasses nature. Instead, he assures her that nothing is impossible for God (Luke 1:37): It is the Holy Spirit who will overshadow and empower her (1:35). Thus, in conceiving and bearing the Son of God, Mary will remain a virgin. This "overshadowing" is the same presence and glory of God that rested on the "dwelling" or "tabernacle"—the portable tent-sanctuary that the Israelites carried with them to house the Ark of the Covenant as they journeyed through the wilderness (Exodus 40:34-35).

Mary must have been in awe as she heard Gabriel describe the child to be so wondrously conceived in her. He is to be named Jesus (Luke 1:31), meaning "The Lord saves." This child whom Mary is asked to bear would be the promised heir of Israel's greatest king, David: "The Lord God will give to him the throne of his father David, and he will reign over the house of Jacob for ever; and of his kingdom there will be no end" (1:32-33).

In these few moments, Mary's future has been unveiled for her. God has, amazingly, asked her to be the mother of Israel's Messiah! St. Bernard of Clairvaux eloquently captures the sense of anticipation as Gabriel awaited Mary's response in his *Homilies in Praise of the Blessed Virgin Mary*:

> Say the word and receive the Word: give yours and conceive God's. Breathe one fleeting word and embrace the everlasting Word. . . . Blessed Virgin, open your heart to faith, your lips to consent and your womb to your Creator. Behold, the long-desired of all nations is standing at the door and knocking. (*Homily IV*, 8)

Although she understands little of what this would mean for her, Mary gives her wholehearted and unreserved assent: "Behold, I am the handmaid of the Lord; let it be to me according to your word" (Luke 1:38).

Mary's consent is not cheap or ill-considered. She was a young woman of Israel, steeped in a knowledge of the prophetic promises God had made to his people and full of eager longing to see them fulfilled. She held God's word and his promises in reverence and based her life on them. So, though she is bewildered and unsure of all the implications of the angel's message, her yes to God rises out of faith in him and in his wisdom and goodness. She takes God at his word and trusts him totally to fulfill it in her and to care for her as she gives herself over to it. She has an unerring conviction that God will honor and meet her consent with grace, help, and protection, supplying her with all she needs to carry it out.

Nor is Mary's *fiat* a "one-time only" consent—it will be repeated over and over in the days and years ahead. It initially opens her to be the recipient of the Word making a home in her. Mary will literally bear the Word of God in the flesh; then she will be borne up by him. Her steady pondering of the word and her constant affirmation of it, repeatedly assenting to God's purposes, will carry her forward in unwavering faith and obedience.

Two thousand years after Mary said yes to God in Nazareth, her example still offers us strength to follow God's will in our own lives. As we stood on the threshold of this new millennium, Pope John Paul II wrote of her:

> Mary, who conceived the Incarnate Word by the power of the Holy Spirit and then in the whole of her life allowed herself to be guided by his interior activity, will be contemplated and imitated . . . above all as the woman who was docile to the voice of the Spirit, a woman of silence and attentiveness, a woman of hope. (*Tertio Millennio Adveniente*, 48)

Pondering the Word

1. Gabriel called Mary "full of grace" (Luke 1:28) and told her that she had "found favor with God" (1:30). The original Greek word *kecharitomene* (translated here as "favor") is related to "grace," indicating that Mary was "graced" by God. What do Gabriel's words imply about the way God prepared Mary for her role as the Mother of God?

_____

_____

_____

_____

_____

_____

_____

_____

_____

2. How did Gabriel describe the child Mary was to bear (Luke 1:31-33, 35)? What might Mary have understood by the titles the angel applied to this child? Read 2 Samuel 7:12-16, Isaiah 9:6-7, and Psalm 89:26-29 to expand your understanding.

_____

_____

_____

_____

_____

_____

_____

_____

3. Note the words and actions of Mary in this scene that indicate how she felt about the angel's greeting and his announcement. What do they reveal about her character? What changes in her emotions and responses do you think she expressed as the conversation with Gabriel progressed?

_____

_____

_____

_____

_____

_____

_____

_____

4. What does Mary's question, "How can this be?" (Luke 1:34), suggest to you about the interplay between faith that seeks for understanding and doubt or unbelief? In what sort of tone or attitude do you think she posed her question?

_____

_____

_____

_____

_____

_____

_____

_____

5. Why do you think Gabriel informed Mary that the elderly Elizabeth, previously barren, was now pregnant (Luke 1:36)? What effect do you think this knowledge had on Mary?

_____

_____

_____

_____

_____

_____

_____

_____

Living the Word

1. When have you felt that God was asking the unimaginable of you? How did you respond to him? What kind of questions or doubts did you raise before God? How can Mary's example help you trust God and his intentions for you?

_____

_____

_____

_____

_____

_____

_____

_____

2. What sorts of "signs" has God given you to strengthen your faith, confirm his word to you, or reassure you of his care? How did you respond to these signs? Can you recall any situation in your life, or in the life of someone you know, where you would say God did the "impossible" (Luke 1:37)? What effect did this have on your faith?

_____

_____

_____

_____

_____

_____

_____

_____

3. Have you ever experienced something surprisingly new and fresh coming to birth in your circumstances once you said yes to God? How different was this from your own expectations and plans?

_____

_____

_____

_____

_____

_____

_____

_____

_____

4. Mary received God's word through the angelic messenger and carried the Word-made-flesh within her. In what ways does God's word come to you? How have you let it "make a home" in you?

_____

_____

_____

_____

_____

_____

_____

_____

5. In what particular situations do you see the Spirit at work in you and in those around you? What role does the Holy Spirit play in your everyday life?

_____

_____

_____

_____

_____

_____

_____

_____

Rooted in the Word

Mary: A Portrait of Trusting Obedience

Mary's assent to God's request is a model to us in many ways: a model for responding to the will of the Father in our lives; for personally welcoming and receiving Jesus; for being open to the action of the Holy Spirit; and for embracing the word of God and allowing it to be implanted in us to grow and bear fruit.

When Mary gave her consent to bear Jesus, the Word was made flesh—literally—from her human substance. Physically, Jesus had her genes. In appearance, perhaps he even "had his mother's eyes" and the same hair color and complexion as hers. Years later, when Jesus declared, "My mother and my brethren are those who hear the word of God and do it" (Luke 8:21), he was not repudiating his family ties or criticizing his mother. Rather, he was commending Mary not only as his mother according to the flesh, but as one who had indeed done the will of God. By pointing to Mary's obedience and trust, Jesus was making it clear that her fundamental relationship with him was not through her physical connection to him but through hearing and acting on the word of God. As St. Augustine expressed it, Mary is more blessed "not because in her womb the Word was made flesh and dwelt among us, but because she kept God's very Word, through whom she was made, and who was made flesh in her" (*Tractate X on the Gospel of John*, 3).

None of us can be united with Jesus in the way that Mary was as his biological mother. But each of us can, like her, embrace him through faith and trust. Through our obedience to his word, we, too, can be closely and intimately united to Jesus as members of his family.

Read and prayerfully reflect on these additional Scripture passages that portray examples of acting in trusting obedience to God:

Sacrifice and offering thou dost not
    desire;
  but thou hast given me an open ear.
Burnt offering and sin offering thou
    hast not required.
Then I said, "Lo, I come;
  in the roll of the book it is written
  of me;
I delight to do thy will, O my God."
(Psalm 40:6-8)

[Jesus] fell on his face and prayed, "My Father, if it be possible, let this cup pass from me; nevertheless, not as I will, but as thou wilt." (Matthew 26:39)

Have this mind among yourselves, which was in Christ Jesus, who, though he was in the form of God, did not count equality with God a thing to be grasped, but emptied himself, taking the form of a servant, being born in the likeness of men. And being found in human form he humbled himself and became obedient unto death, even death on a cross. (Philippians 2:5-8)

By faith Abraham obeyed when he was called to go out to a place which he was to receive as an inheritance; and he went out, not knowing where he was to go. By faith he sojourned in the land of promise, as in a foreign land, living in tents with Isaac and Jacob, heirs with him of the same promise. For he looked forward to the city which has foundations, whose builder and maker is God. (Hebrews 11:8-10)

Rebekah: Another Portrait of Trusting Obedience

Read Genesis 24

The Old Testament's story of Rebekah resembles the Annunciation scene in several ways. In Luke's account, God sent Gabriel, his servant, to Mary to gain her consent to bear his Son. In Genesis, Abraham sent his servant to find a wife for his son Isaac. In both instances, the consent of the woman allowed God's plan of salvation to further unfold.

Rebekah went willingly with Abraham's servant to her future husband (Genesis 24:58).

Like Mary, she made a free choice, trusting God in what she recognized as his invitation and purpose for her life. As Isaac's wife, Rebekah became the mother of Jacob and the grandmother of Judah—from whose tribe the Messiah was descended. Through their trust and obedience, both Rebekah and Mary became key links in Christ's genealogy.

We see the mystery of God's action in Rebekah and Mary: Each gave her consent freely, yet it was given in response to God's grace. We, too, can rely on God for the grace that prepares us to embrace his will.

Treasuring the Word

A Reading from *The Reed of God* by Caryll Houselander

Fiat

To what was [Mary] asked to consent?

First of all, to the descent of the Holy Spirit, to surrender her littleness to the Infinite Love, and as a result to become the Mother of Christ.

It was so tremendous, yet so passive.

She was not asked to do anything herself, but to let something be done to her.

She was not asked to lead a special kind of life, to retire to the temple and live as a nun, to cultivate suitable virtues or claim special privileges.

She was simply to remain in the world, to go forward with her marriage to Joseph, to live the life of an artisan's wife, just what she had planned to do when she had no idea that anything out of the ordinary would ever happen to her.

It almost seemed as if God's becoming man and being born of a woman *were* ordinary. . . .

Outwardly [Mary's daily life] would not differ from the life she would have led if she had not been chosen to be the Bride of the Spirit and the Mother of God at all!

She was not even asked to live it alone with this God who was her own Being and whose Being was to be hers.

No, He asked for her ordinary life shared with Joseph. She was not to neglect her simple human tenderness, her love for an earthly man, because God was her unborn child.

On the contrary, the hands and feet, the heart, the waking, sleeping and eating that were forming Christ were to form Him in service to Joseph.

Yes, it certainly seemed that God wanted to give the world the impression that it is ordinary for Him to be born of a human creature.

Well, that is a fact. God did mean it to be the ordinary thing, for it is His will that Christ shall be born in every human being's life and not, as a rule, through extraordinary things, but through the ordinary daily life and the human love that people give to one another.

Our Lady said yes.

She said yes for us all. . . .

Our Lady said yes for the human race. Each one of us must echo that yes for our own lives.

We are all asked if we will surrender what we are, our humanity, our flesh and blood, to the Holy Spirit and allow Christ to fill the emptiness formed by the particular shape of our life.

The surrender that is asked of us includes complete and absolute trust; it must be like Our Lady's surrender, without condition and without reservation. . . .

What we shall be asked to give is our flesh and blood, our daily life—our thoughts, our service to one another, our affections and loves, our words, our intellect, our waking, working and sleeping, our ordinary human joys and sorrows—to God.

To surrender all that we are, as we are, to the Spirit of Love in order that our lives may bear Christ into the world—that is what we shall be asked.

Our Lady has made this possible. Her *fiat* was for herself and for us, but if we want God's will to be completed in us as it is in her, we must echo her *fiat*.

The Visitation

Blessed is she who believed that there would be a fulfillment of what was spoken to her from the Lord.
Luke 1:45

The time of pregnancy is for Mary a time of perfect contemplation, of exhaustive listening to the Son. But at the same time it is a time of action, for she goes to Elizabeth to bring her the Son, to pass on the gift that she has received from God.
Adrienne von Speyr,
Handmaid of the Lord

Visitation Day

In haste Mary climbed the hills of Judah,
a young girl
hurried by the secret growing in her
to seek reassurance
from another who
also held in quiet confidence
the certainty that nothing is impossible with God.

And Elizabeth did not fail her:
Blessed are you among women,
and blessed is the fruit of your womb.
The Spirit prompted her
to instant recognition
of Mary's hidden treasure
as her own babe leapt within her womb,
already eager to commence his herald role.

Then Mary spilled her joy
(forever scattering grace about her)
in words that long millennia
have never silenced.
And all generations since that Visitation Day
have called her blessed
as they too magnify the Word
so wondrously clothed in this virgin's flesh.

1:39 In those days Mary arose and went with haste into the hill country, to a city of Judah, 40 and she entered the house of Zechariah and greeted Elizabeth. 41 And when Elizabeth heard the greeting of Mary, the babe leaped in her womb; and Elizabeth was filled with the Holy Spirit 42 and she exclaimed with a loud cry, "Blessed are you among women, and blessed is the fruit of your womb! 43 And why is this granted me, that the mother of my Lord should come to me? 44 For behold, when the voice of your greeting came to my ears, the babe in my womb leaped for joy. 45 And blessed is she who believed that there would be a fulfillment of what was spoken to her from the Lord." 46 And Mary said,

> "My soul magnifies the Lord,
> 47 and my spirit rejoices in God my Savior,
> 48 for he has regarded the low estate of his handmaiden.
> For behold, henceforth all generations will call me blessed;

> 49 for he who is mighty has done great things for me,
> and holy is his name.
> 50 And his mercy is on those who fear him from generation to generation.
> 51 He has shown strength with his arm, he has scattered the proud in the imagination of their hearts,
> 52 he has put down the mighty from their thrones,
> and exalted those of low degree;
> 53 he has filled the hungry with good things,
> and the rich he has sent empty away.
> 54 He has helped his servant Israel, in remembrance of his mercy,
> 55 as he spoke to our fathers, to Abraham and to his posterity for ever."

56 And Mary remained with her about three months, and returned to her home.

Reflecting on the Word

After giving her *fiat*, "let it be to me according to your word," Mary hurriedly sets out to visit Elizabeth (Luke 1:38-39). She is eager to confide her fears and confusion as well as her joy and wonder at the angel's strange message to this kinswoman who she hopes will accept the miraculous. For hadn't the angel told her that Elizabeth, childless and well past her childbearing years, is now six months pregnant (1:36)?

Though Scripture is silent on this point, most likely Mary did not make this long trip by herself since it was not the custom for women in first-century Palestine to travel alone. Might we imagine that it was her father, or her betrothed, Joseph, who accompanied her? On this journey, Mary carried the Word incarnate within her as she passed through the hill country of Judea. Like her, we are to carry God's word with us through the mountains and valleys of daily life.

In most cultures, including the Jewish one, a young woman would be the one to greet her elder with respect. However, on this occasion, it is Elizabeth who honors Mary. First, in calling Mary "blessed" (Luke 1:42), the older woman recognizes that the younger has been chosen by God—Mary is not great by any achievement of her own but rather by God's choice. Second, Elizabeth honors Mary because she is to bear a special child. In societies ruled by kings, honor is accorded to the mothers of kings because they gave birth to them.

How much greater honor is due to the mother of the Lord! Finally, Elizabeth lauds her cousin because of her faith: "Blessed is she who believed that there would be a fulfillment of what was spoken to her from the Lord" (1:45).

In this homey scene, Mary and Elizabeth rejoice together in the coming births of their children. But this is not only a happy meeting between two mothers-to-be, but also a meeting between their sons. Something profound is taking place in this scene: the first responses that human beings make to the human presence of God among them.

At Mary's approach, Elizabeth's own child leaps in her womb in recognition of this presence. Thus, even before his birth, John the Baptist begins his lifelong mission to proclaim the coming of the Messiah and prepare the way for him. Later the Holy Spirit— whose continual work is to reveal the presence of God in the world—will again point out the Messiah to John (see John 1:33-34).

Seventeenth-century Cardinal Pierre de Bérulle, a friend of St. Francis de Sales, was known as the "Apostle of the Incarnate Word" because of his many writing on the life of Jesus. Reflecting on John's first encounter with the incarnate Christ, de Bérulle wrote:

> God has become a child, and so he wants first to be known and adored by a child . . . God is a child, the world ignores, heaven adores, and a child is the first person in the universe to recognize

and adore him, and he does so by the homage and secret operation of God himself, who wants to act upon children. He wants to honor himself as child by giving the first knowledge of himself to a child in the world, making him his prophet in the universe. (*Opuscules de pieté*)

Then, filled with the Spirit, Elizabeth becomes the first to honor the Lord in his human nature when she calls the fruit of Mary's womb "blessed" (Luke 1:41-42). Perhaps it was also Elizabeth's awareness of God's recent graciousness to her and Zechariah—she is now pregnant after so many years of infertility—that increased her sensitivity to God's action in others. She recognizes how privileged she is to encounter God so personally: "Why is this granted me, that the mother of my Lord should come to me?" (1:43).

Mary's beautiful hymn of gratitude to God springs from her heart as—perhaps in relief at her warm welcome—she responds to Elizabeth's greeting. Mary has no illusions about herself or her own worthiness. She does not confuse God's choice of her with any merit of her own. Rather, as St. Bede the Venerable noted, "She refers all her greatness to the gift of the one whose essence is power and whose nature is greatness, for he fills with greatness and strength the small and the weak who believe in him" (*Homily IV*). Mary recognizes that she is unworthy of the honor bestowed on her and takes no glory for herself: "He has regarded the low estate of his handmaiden. . . . He who is mighty has done great things for me, and holy is his name" (Luke 1:48-49).

Mary also "magnifies" the Lord, praising him for his mercy and compassion on the lowly—a mercy she knows to be based on his word and on the covenant love he pledged to Abraham and his people so long ago (Luke 1:54-55). Future generations will call Mary blessed (1:48) because she recognized, cooperated with, and proclaimed the glory of God working in her.

In traveling to her cousin, Mary also generously anticipates the elderly Elizabeth's need for help during the last months of her pregnancy. Thus, Mary spends the first trimester of her own pregnancy supporting her older cousin (Luke 1:56). Her days of waiting and preparing herself inwardly for the birth of her son are passed in humbly serving Elizabeth.

Pondering the Word

1. What do Elizabeth's words to Mary indicate about Elizabeth's relationship with God? About Elizabeth's own character? What are the main points that Elizabeth makes?

_____

_____

_____

_____

_____

_____

_____

_____

_____

2. What do you think Elizabeth's greeting meant to Mary? Notice that Elizabeth is the first person in Scripture to call Mary "mother of my Lord" (Luke 1:43). How did Elizabeth recognize this?

_____

_____

_____

_____

_____

_____

_____

_____

_____

3. The Greek verb *skirtao* describing John's "leap" in his mother's womb (Luke 1:41, 44) is the same word used to describe David dancing in front of the Ark of the Covenant where the Israelites housed God's written word (2 Samuel 6:14-16). What does John's action suggest about his future character and role?

_____

_____

_____

_____

_____

_____

_____

_____

4. What phrases and adjectives does Mary use in her canticle of praise to describe God and his actions toward her? To describe herself? What do her words reveal about her attitude toward God? Toward herself?

_____

_____

_____

_____

_____

_____

_____

_____

5. Mary's prayer was rooted in Scripture. Look at some of the many Old Testament passages that are reflected in the *Magnificat*, such as 1 Samuel 2:1-10, Psalm 34:2-3, and Psalm 138:6. What do these additional texts tell you about God? About his faithfulness to his promises?

_____

_____

_____

_____

_____

_____

_____

_____

_____

Living the Word

1. In what ways do you recognize the hidden presence of Jesus around you? How do you respond to this presence? What can you do to make your conversations reflect God's presence?

_____

_____

_____

_____

_____

_____

_____

_____

_____

2. Mary and Elizabeth rejoiced with one another over the different ways God had blessed them. How do you react when you see others blessed by God?

_____

_____

_____

_____

_____

_____

_____

_____

_____

3. Elizabeth was moved by the Holy Spirit to honor Mary. How do you express your love for Mary? In what ways do you honor her? Ask the Holy Spirit to inspire and guide you so that your relationship with Mary deepens and grows.

_____

_____

_____

_____

_____

_____

_____

_____

_____

4. How do some ways in which you are living your life bring glory to God? Make up your own prayer of praise glorifying God for his actions in your life.

_____

_____

_____

_____

_____

_____

_____

_____

_____

5. Reflect on Mary and Elizabeth in their love and humility toward one another. Consider how you can reach out and serve someone in need the way Mary served Elizabeth.

_____

_____

_____

_____

_____

_____

_____

_____

_____

Rooted in the Word

Mary: A Portrait of Faith

As a faithful daughter of Israel, Mary cherished the prophetic promises God made to his people and longed to see them fulfilled. She looked forward to the coming of the Messiah with hopeful expectation. When God singled her out and asked her to play a key role in his plan, she took him at his word and gave herself over to it in trust.

Mary's *fiat* was an act of faith in God—faith that allowed God's word to be fulfilled in her and literally become through her the Word-made-flesh. In the Visitation scene, Elizabeth honored Mary for the faith she placed in the message God had spoken to her (Luke 1:45).

Through Jesus' coming into the world as a human being, men and women enter into direct, personal contact with God himself. This coming also brings us into deeper contact with one another as we share our encounters with Jesus. When Christ's coming brought Mary and Elizabeth together, the two encouraged and strengthened each other as they believed in God's promises. Faith, hope, and love grew stronger in them through this encounter with one another and with God in their midst.

Read and prayerfully reflect on these additional Scripture passages that express faith in God and its fruit:

In hope [Abraham] believed against hope, that he should become the father of many nations; as he had been told, "So shall your descendants be." He did not weaken in faith when he considered his own body, which was as good as dead because he was about a hundred years old, or when he considered the barrenness of Sarah's womb. No distrust made him waver concerning the promise of God, but he grew strong in his faith as he gave glory to God, fully convinced that God was able to do what he had promised. (Romans 4:18-21)

Faith is the assurance of things hoped for, the conviction of things not seen. For by it the men of old received divine approval. (Hebrews 11:1-2)

You know that the testing of your faith produces steadfastness. And let steadfastness have its full effect, that you may be perfect and complete, lacking in nothing. (James 1:3-4)

Without having seen him you love him; though you do not now see him you believe in him and rejoice with unutterable and exalted joy. As the outcome of your faith you obtain the salvation of your souls. (1 Peter 1:8-9)

Hannah: Another Portrait of Faith

Read 1 Samuel 1:1–2:10

Hannah, like the barren Sarah and Elizabeth, conceived a child after long years of hopeful prayer. Ultimately, her faith was rewarded and she bore a son, whom she named Samuel because, as she said, "I have asked him of the LORD" (1 Samuel 1:20).

Hannah, like Mary, gave herself and her child to God fully, so that his word might be established (1 Samuel 1:23). She did not hold on to her son or to her own desires and ideas for his future, but freely returned him to God: "For this child I prayed; and the LORD has granted me my petition which I made to him. Therefore I have lent him to the LORD; as long as he lives, he is lent to the LORD" (1:27-28). Mary, too, would learn to give up her son to God's purposes.

Finally, Mary's *Magnificat* resembles Hannah's hymn of praise. Both women recall God's faithfulness to his covenant and promises, praise him for his mercy, and reflect on their own humility and God's blessings on the lowly.

Treasuring the Word

A Reading from Pope John Paul II's General Audience
of October 2, 1996

The Visitation Is a Prelude to Jesus' Mission

In the visitation episode, St. Luke shows how the grace of the Incarnation, after filling Mary, brings salvation and joy to Elizabeth's house. Carried in his Mother's womb, the Savior of men pours out the Holy Spirit, revealing himself from the start of his coming into the world. In describing Mary's departure for Judea, the evangelist uses the verb *anístemi*, which means "to arise," "to start moving." Considering that this verb is used in the Gospels to indicate Jesus' resurrection (Mark 8:31; 9:9, 31; Luke 24:7, 46) or physical actions that imply a spiritual effort (Luke 5:27-28; 15:18, 20), we can suppose that Luke wishes to stress with this expression the vigorous zeal which led Mary, under the inspiration of the Holy Spirit, to give to the world its Savior.

The Gospel text also reports that Mary made the journey "with haste" (Luke 1:39). In the Lucan context, even the note "into the hill country" (1:39) appears to be much more than a simple topographical indication, since it calls to mind the messenger of good news described in the Book of Isaiah: "How beautiful upon the mountains are the feet of him who brings good tidings, who announces peace, who bears good news, who announces salvation, who says to Zion: 'Your God reigns'" (Isaiah 52:7).

Like St. Paul, who recognized the fulfillment of this prophetic text in the preaching of the Gospel (Romans 10:15), St. Luke also seems to invite us to see Mary as the first "evangelist," who spreads the "good news," initiating the missionary journeys of her divine Son. Lastly, the direction of the Blessed Virgin's journey is particularly significant: it will be from Galilee to Judea, like Jesus' missionary journey (cf. 9:51). Mary's visit to Elizabeth is a prelude to Jesus' mission, and in cooperating from the beginning of her motherhood in the Son's redeeming work, she became the model of those in the Church who set out to bring Christ's light and joy to the people of every time and place. . . .

St. Luke relates that "when Elizabeth heard the greeting of Mary, the babe leaped in her womb" (Luke 1:41). Mary's greeting caused Elizabeth's son to leap for joy. Jesus' entrance into Elizabeth's house, at Mary's doing, brought the unborn prophet that gladness which the Old Testament foretells as a sign of the Messiah's presence. At

Mary's greeting, messianic joy came over Elizabeth too, and "filled with the Holy Spirit . . . she exclaimed with a loud cry, 'Blessed are you among women, and blessed is the fruit of your womb!'" (Luke 1:41-42). By a higher light, she understood Mary's greatness: more than Jael (Judges 5:24-31) and Judith (Judith 8:32-33; 13:18-20), who prefigured her in the Old Testament, she is blessed among women because of the fruit of her womb, Jesus the Messiah. . . .

In view of Mary's excellence, Elizabeth also understood what an honor this visit was for her: "And why is this granted me, that the mother of my Lord should come to me?" (Luke 1:43). With the expression "my Lord," Elizabeth recognized the royal messianic dignity of Mary's Son. In the Old Testament this expression was used to address the king (cf. 1 Kings 1:13, 20, 21, etc.) and used to speak of the Messiah King (Psalm 110:1). The angel had said of Jesus: "The Lord God will give to him the throne of his father David" (Luke 1:32). "Filled with the Holy Spirit," Elizabeth had the same insight. Later, the paschal glorification of Christ would reveal the sense in which this title is to be understood, that is, a transcendent sense (cf. John 20:28; Acts 2:34-36).

With her admiring exclamation, Elizabeth invites us to appreciate all that the Virgin's presence brings as a gift to the life of every believer. In the visitation, the Virgin brought Christ to the Baptist's mother, the Christ who pours out the Holy Spirit. This role of mediatrix is brought out by Elizabeth's very words: "For behold, when the voice of your greeting came to my ears, the babe in my womb leaped for joy" (Luke 1:44). By the gift of the Holy Spirit, Mary's presence serves as a prelude to Pentecost, confirming a cooperation which, having begun with the Incarnation, is destined to be expressed in the whole work of divine salvation.

The Nativity

And [Mary] gave birth to her first-born son and wrapped him in swaddling cloths, and laid him in a manger, because there was no place for them in the inn.
Luke 2:7

His Mother carried him in her womb, may we carry him in our hearts; the Virgin became pregnant with the Incarnation of Christ, may our hearts become pregnant with faith in Christ; she brought forth the Savior, may our souls bring forth salvation and praise. May our souls be not sterile, but fertile for God.
St. Augustine, *Sermons, 189, 3*

The Road to Bethlehem

What relief had been Mary's
when Joseph's light-filled eyes and gentle smile
had let her know that he, too, had received the angel's message!

And in the quiet months that followed,
how the two must have wondered
and pondered the ancient prophecies,
searching for understanding to ease the questions in their hearts.
Had they dared to voice their hidden fears and sense of awe,
or were they calmly silent
because it was enough for them to know
they could rest secure in God's will?
Had they knelt together in humble prayer before their God,
preparing their hearts to receive the child so wondrously
(and so miraculously)
to be entrusted to their care and keeping?

And then the waiting had been interrupted by Rome's decree
and the two made ready
and set off upon the road to David's city.
Did Mary fret a bit as she packed,
wondering whether to take the swaddling bands
and little garments she had stitched—
or would they be back home again in their own village
before her time had come?
Did Joseph cast a last look longingly back over his shoulder
as Nazareth's security passed out of sight?

Yet the same road that led far from familiarity and comfort
led straightway to the city of promise:

42

You, O Bethlehem Ephrathah,
who are little to be among the clans of Judah,
from you shall come forth for me
one who is to be ruler in Israel,
whose origin is from of old,
from ancient days.

Joseph set a steady pace, careful of his young wife's comfort,
but eager to put the road behind them—
eager to arrive and find a place where she could rest
while he went about the business of being counted by Caesar,
then finally
eager to be on the way home again with Mary.
But that was not to be.

How Joseph's heart must have troubled him
as he sought in vain among the crowded streets to find shelter
for God's coming in the flesh.

And she gave birth to her first-born son
and wrapped him in swaddling clothes, and laid him in a manger,
because there was no place for them in the inn.

Yes, Mary bound the child in swaddling bands
that our binding sins might be loosed
and laid him in the feed-trough upon the hay—
he who was to become crushed wheat and life-giving bread
to fill our hearts' hunger.

Matthew 1:18-25

1:18 Now the birth of Jesus Christ took place in this way. When his mother Mary had been betrothed to Joseph, before they came together she was found to be with child of the Holy Spirit; 19 and her husband Joseph, being a just man and unwilling to put her to shame, resolved to divorce her quietly. 20 But as he considered this, behold, an angel of the Lord appeared to him in a dream, saying, "Joseph, son of David, do not fear to take Mary your wife, for that which is conceived in her is of the Holy Spirit; 21 she will bear a son, and you shall call his name Jesus, for he will save his people from their sins." 22 All this took place to fulfill what the Lord had spoken by the prophet:

23 "Behold, a virgin shall conceive and bear a son,

and his name shall be called Emmanuel" (which means, God with us). 24 When Joseph woke from sleep, he did as the angel of the Lord commanded him; he took his wife, 25 but knew her not until she had borne a son; and he called his name Jesus.

2:1 In those days a decree went out from Caesar Augustus that all the world should be enrolled. 2 This was the first enrollment, when Quirinius was governor of Syria. 3 And all went to be enrolled, each to his own city. 4 And Joseph also went up from Galilee, from the city of Nazareth, to Judea, to the city of David, which is called Bethlehem, because he was of the house and lineage of David, 5 to be enrolled with Mary, his betrothed, who was with child. 6 And while they were there, the time came for her to be delivered. 7 And she gave birth to her first-born son and wrapped him in swaddling cloths, and laid him in a manger, because there was no place for them in the inn.

8 And in that region there were shepherds out in the field, keeping watch over their flock by night. 9 And an angel of the Lord appeared to them, and the glory of the Lord shone around them, and they were filled with fear. 10 And the angel said to them, "Be not afraid; for behold, I bring you good news of a great joy which will come to all the people; 11 for to you is born this day in the city of David a Savior, who is Christ the Lord. 12 And this will be a sign for you: you will find a babe wrapped in swaddling cloths and lying in a manger." 13 And suddenly there was with the angel a multitude of the heavenly host praising God and saying,

14 "Glory to God in the highest,
and on earth peace among men with whom
he is pleased!"

15 When the angels went away from them into heaven, the shepherds said to one another, "Let us go over to Bethlehem and see this thing that has happened, which the Lord has made known to us." 16 And they went with haste, and found Mary and Joseph, and the babe lying in a manger. 17 And when they saw it they made known the saying which had been told them concerning this child; 18 and all who heard it wondered at what the shepherds told them. 19 But Mary kept all these things, pondering them in her heart. 20 And the shepherds returned, glorifying and praising God for all they had heard and seen, as it had been told them.

21 And at the end of eight days, when he was circumcised, he was called Jesus, the name given by the angel before he was conceived in the womb.

Reflecting on the Word

Israel's long wait is finally rewarded. The time God had designated to unveil his plan of salvation in the person of Jesus is now here: "When the time had fully come, God sent forth his Son, born of woman, born under the law, to redeem those who were under the law, so that we might receive adoption as sons" (Galatians 4:4-5).

Imagine Joseph's perplexity and anguish as he realizes that his betrothed is pregnant. Did Mary remain silent as she held the secret knowledge of the Word growing within her, hoping that God himself would reveal this mystery to Joseph? Did she tremble in her innocence as she thought of her fiancé's pain and waited for his response? Surely Mary grieved at what he might think of her.

Joseph wrestles with himself, wanting neither to take Mary as his wife nor subject her to a shameful trial as a woman suspected of adultery. Then he resolves not to marry his betrothed (Matthew 1:19). But God intervenes—and again speaks through an angelic messenger. Like Mary, Joseph is invited to participate in God's surprising plan of salvation. The angel tells him not to fear to take Mary as his wife, assuring him of the divine purpose at work in her (1:20). Moreover, Joseph is entrusted with the responsibility of naming the child (1:21, 25), an act indicating legal paternity and insuring that Jesus is adopted into Joseph's lineage, the house of David.

Matthew does not record any words of Joseph in reply to the angel. Joseph gives his response simply in his obedience, doing as he is instructed (1:24). By marrying Mary, he expresses his own "let it be done to me according to your word." His response to God's revelation provides a normal family environment for the birth and raising of this special child. As Mary's husband and Jesus' foster father, Joseph safeguards their honor and establishes a secure and happy home. The angel's message in the dream was only the prelude to Joseph's lifelong relationship with Jesus as father to son.

With words of great simplicity, Luke's account of the Nativity describes the most awesome act of love that we could ever imagine: God himself takes on human flesh! Our human intellects are bewildered when we try to grasp what Jesus did in the Incarnation. As the theologian Romano Guardini wrote:

> Let us consider carefully what this means: that the everlasting, infinite creator not only reigns over or in the world but, at a specific "moment," crossed an unimaginable borderline and personally entered into history. . . . Once at this point a friend gave me a clue that helped my understanding more than any measure of bare reason. He said, "But love does such things!" (*The Lord*)

The shepherds are astonished when their normal watch over their flock is interrupted by the appearance of an angel (Luke 2:8-9)! Yet it is fitting that the ordinary is interrupted by an extraordinary messenger as the most extraordinary event of all human history occurs. On that night, heaven and earth are joined together in responding to the birth of Christ as an angelic host sings "Glory to God in the highest" and the shepherds rush to Bethlehem to witness the wonder that had been proclaimed to them (Luke 2:14-16).

After the shepherds tell Mary and Joseph what they had learned from the angel about this child, they return to their flocks, "glorifying and praising God for all they had heard and seen" (Luke 2:17, 20). With the birth of Jesus, new hope breaks forth in the dull monotony of their days. The memory of this wonder-filled night will remain with the shepherds throughout their lives, giving them the satisfaction and comfort of knowing that a child is growing up to be their Savior.

How bewildered yet reassured Mary and Joseph must have been by the unexpected visit of these simple men! Now they are no longer the only ones who have been visited by angels foretelling awesome things about their child. While all who hear the shepherds' report wonder at their words, the mother's response is deeper and enduring: "Mary kept all these things, pondering them in her heart" (Luke 2:17-19).

Mary will treasure all these strange events through the years ahead, turning them over and over in her mind like a gemstone cutter turning a fine diamond around and around, letting the light play on each facet to reveal its beauty. God's unlikely plan of salvation is now unfolding—and Mary is inextricably caught up in it.

Pondering the Word

1. What does Joseph's reaction to Mary's unexpected pregnancy suggest to you about his character? What does the angel tell Joseph about the child Mary is carrying? Do you think Joseph understood this? What was Joseph's role in God's plan?

_____

_____

_____

_____

_____

_____

_____

_____

2. By being given the responsibility to name Jesus, Joseph, son of David, became Jesus' legal father (Matthew 1:21, 25). What does this mean for Jesus' lineage (see also Matthew's genealogy of Jesus in 1:1-16)? What do you think Joseph's relationship with Jesus was like as Jesus was growing up?

_____

_____

_____

_____

_____

_____

_____

_____

3. Note the information that Luke gives about the circumstances of Christ's birth, such as Augustus' census, the city of David, and the manger. What is the significance of these details? What does the coming of Christ into this physical setting and world milieu say to you?

_____

_____

_____

_____

_____

_____

_____

_____

_____

4. The angel's message to the shepherds called Jesus a savior (Luke 2:11). What does the title "Savior" mean to you? See John 4:42; Acts 4:10, 12; 2 Timothy 1:10; and Titus 2:11-14 to expand your understanding.

_____

_____

_____

_____

_____

_____

_____

_____

5. Just as the infant Jesus at birth was "wrapped . . . in swaddling cloths, and laid in a manger, because there was no place for them in the inn" (Luke 2:7), the dead body of Jesus was "wrapped . . . in a linen shroud, and laid . . . in a rock-hewn tomb, where no one had ever yet been laid" (23:53). What do these parallels suggest to you?

_____

_____

_____

_____

_____

_____

_____

_____

_____

6. Picture the shepherds' visit to Mary and Joseph (Luke 2:16-20) and imagine the conversation between them. How do you think this event affected Mary?

_____

_____

_____

_____

_____

_____

_____

_____

_____

Living the Word

1. Joseph was a man who trusted and obeyed God, and God was pleased to entrust him with great responsibility for his Son and for Mary. (Pope John Paul II has called Joseph "Guardian of the Redeemer.") What can you learn from Joseph's example?

_____

_____

_____

_____

_____

_____

_____

_____

_____

_____

2. What do the names "Jesus" and "Emmanuel" mean to you personally? How can reverencing Jesus' name and using this name to speak to him help you when you pray?

_____

_____

_____

_____

_____

_____

_____

_____

_____

_____

3. The trip to Bethlehem for the census seemed to come at a most inconvenient time for Mary and Joseph, yet it fulfilled God's purpose. When did you ever have difficulty with God's timing? How did you deal with it?

_____

_____

_____

_____

_____

_____

_____

_____

4. What might you do to renew your appreciation of Christ's Incarnation and to express your gratitude for it? Imagine yourself in the place of the shepherds returning from Bethlehem, "glorifying and praising God for all they had heard and seen" (Luke 2:20). Then write your own prayer of praise to God.

_____

_____

_____

_____

_____

_____

_____

_____

5. Mary held all the strange events surrounding her son's birth in her memory, "pondering them in her heart" (Luke 2:19). How do you treasure your memories of how God has worked in your life? How often do you reflect on them and seek to understand his purposes for you?

_____

_____

_____

_____

_____

_____

_____

_____

_____

Rooted in the Word

Mary: A Portrait of Motherhood

Passing on *life*—whose source is in God alone—from one generation to the next is among the most profound of human experiences. When a woman becomes a mother, she is linked in a unique way to the Creator of all life. In the Nativity we see the unique identity of Mary as the mother of Jesus. Mary's motherhood, the fruit of the Spirit's overshadowing, is a mystery and a paradox: In conceiving and giving birth, she remains a virgin yet becomes mother of a baby—and of God himself!

As a mother cares for her infant in its helplessness and dependency, Mary cared for all the human needs of her divine child. Imagine her cradling Jesus in her arms, giving him her breast to nurse, and looking lovingly upon this child. Pope John Paul II reflected on the wonder of Mary's motherhood and the bond between this unique mother and her son:

> The contemplation of Christ has an *incomparable model* in Mary. In a unique way the face of the Son belongs to Mary. It was in her womb that Christ was formed, receiving from her a human resemblance which points to an even greater spiritual closeness. No one has ever devoted himself to the contemplation of the face of Christ as faithfully as Mary. (*Rosarium Virginis Mariae*, 10)

Read and prayerfully reflect on these additional Scripture passages that describe the life-giving nature of God and the essence of motherhood:

> The LORD God formed man of dust from the ground, and breathed into his nostrils the breath of life; and man became a living being. . . . Then the LORD God said, "It is not good that the man should be alone; I will make him a helper fit for him.". . . So the LORD God caused a deep sleep to fall upon man, and while he slept took one of his ribs and closed up its place with flesh; and the rib which the LORD God had taken from the man he made into a woman and brought her to the man. Then the man said, "This at last is bone of my bones and flesh of my flesh; she shall be called Woman, because she was taken out of Man." Therefore a man leaves his father and his mother and cleaves to his wife, and they become one flesh. . . . The man called his wife's name Eve, because she was the mother of all living. (Genesis 2:7, 18, 21-23; 3:20)

54

Now Adam knew Eve his wife, and she conceived and bore Cain, saying, "I have gotten a man with the help of the LORD." (Genesis 4:1)

Thus says the LORD: "Can a woman forget her sucking child, that she should have no compassion on the son of her womb? Even these may forget, yet I will not forget you. Behold, I have graven you on the palms of my hands." (Isaiah 49:15-16)

"Shall I bring to the birth and not cause to bring forth? says the LORD; shall I, who cause to bring forth, shut the womb? says your God." (Isaiah 66:9)

Eve: Another Portrait of Motherhood

Read Genesis 3

When God created a "helper fit for him" (Genesis 2:18), Adam called his wife Eve, "because she was the mother of all living" (3:20). Yet ironically, it was Eve, mother of the human race, who along with her husband brought death to us.

However, when our first parents disobeyed him, God promised to reverse the consequences of sin, giving a hint of hope of the redemption to come: Eve's offspring would crush the serpent and triumph over Satan (Genesis 3:15). This promise was fulfilled through Jesus Christ, born of Mary: "When the time had fully come, God sent forth his Son, born of a woman, born under the law, to redeem those who were under the law, so that we might receive adoption as sons" (Galatians 4:4-5).

The early Church Fathers often compared Eve with Mary. St. Irenaeus wrote, "The knot of Eve's disobedience was untied by Mary's obedience; what the virgin Eve bound through her unbelief, the Virgin Mary loosened by her faith" (*Against Heresies*, III, 22). St. Jerome asserted, "Death through Eve, life through Mary" (*Letters*, 22, 21).

Eve, by her sin, injured the glory of her motherhood. In contrast, it was particularly as a mother that Mary played a unique role in the salvation of humankind: We who were "dead through our trespasses" (Ephesians 2:5) receive new life in and through Christ, Mary' son.

Treasuring the Word

A Reading from *Mary, Mirror of the Church* by Raniero Cantalamessa, O.F.M. Cap.

Mary, Mother of God

It was at Christmas, in fact, and not before, at the moment in which "she gave birth to her first-born son" (Luke 2:7), that Mary truly and fully became the Mother of God. The title "mother" is not like any other title that can be given to a person without, however, affecting the very being of the person. To become a mother, a woman goes through a series of experiences that leave their mark forever and modify not only her physical appearance but her very awareness of herself. It is one of those things that takes place once and forever. At the moment of ordination, we were told, "Once a priest, a priest forever," because of the character that ordination impresses on the soul, according to Catholic doctrine. This is even more true of a woman: once a mother, a mother forever. In this case the character is not the invisible mark left by the event on the soul; it is a creature, a child, destined to live eternally beside its mother and to proclaim her such.

When talking of Mary, Scripture constantly stresses two fundamental acts, or moments, which correspond to what common human experience considers essential for a real and full maternity to take place—to conceive and to give birth. "Behold," the angel said to Mary, "you will conceive in your womb and bear a son" (Luke 1:31). These two moments also exist in Matthew's account: that which was conceived in her was of the Holy Spirit, and she would bear a son (see Matthew 1:20 f.). The prophecy of Isaiah in which all of this had been foretold used the same expression: A "young women shall conceive and bear a son" (Isaiah 7:14). Now you can see why I said that it was only at Christmas, when Mary gave birth to Jesus, that she became in a full sense the Mother of God. The title "Mother of God" (*Dei Genitrix*), used by the Latin Church, places more emphasis on the first of the two moments, on the moment of the conception; whereas the title *Theotokos*, used by the Greek Church, places greater emphasis on the second stage, on the giving birth (*tikto* in Greek means "I am giving birth"). The first moment, the conception, is common to both the father and the mother, while the second, the giving birth, belongs exclusively to the mother.

Mother of God: a title that expresses one of the greatest mysteries and, for human reason, one of the greatest paradoxes in Christianity. It is a title that has filled the liturgy of the Church with wonder. The Church, recalling the moment when the glory of God came in a cloud to dwell in the temple (see 1 Kings 8:27), exclaims: "That which the heavens cannot contain, has become man in your womb!" The title "Mother of God" is Mary's oldest and most important dogmatic title, since at the Council of Ephesus in 431 it was defined by the Church as a truth of faith to be believed by all Christians. It is the basis of all Mary's greatness. It is the principle itself of Mariology. Because of it, Mary is not just an object of devotion in Christianity but also an object of theology, and that means that she is part of the discourse on God himself, because God is directly involved in the divine maternity of Mary. It is also the most ecumenical of her titles, not just historically because it was defined in an ecumenical council, but also practically, because it is the only title shared and accepted without distinction, at least in principle, by all Christian denominations.

The Presentation

A sword will pierce through your own soul also.
Luke 2:35

The Mother of God, the most pure Virgin, carried the true light in her arms and brought him to those who lay in darkness. We too should carry a light for all to see and reflect the radiance of the true light as we hasten to meet him.
St. Sophronius, *Discourse 3 on the Presentation*

Anna's Heir

I stand, Lord, keeping eager watch
as Anna did in distant times before me,
filling the full measure of her years
secluded in the temple
in adoring expectation.

Now I am heir to her post,
a sentinel
still waiting through the long darkness
for the dawn of your return.

All my longing is for you, O Lord,
as I stand poised on tiptoe,
straining with my whole being
to catch that first glimpse of you.

Shatter the darkness
(oft times threatening to close in and surround us)
with that fierce and burning brightness
of your splendor and your beauty.

Then I shall follow Anna's suit
and raise my voice to you in glad thanks
and tell of your redemption
to all who've yearned so long for you.

2:22 And when the time came for their purification according to the law of Moses, [Mary and Joseph] brought him up to Jerusalem to present him to the Lord 23 (as it is written in the law of the Lord, "Every male that opens the womb shall be called holy to the Lord") 24 and to offer a sacrifice according to what is said in the law of the Lord, "a pair of turtledoves, or two young pigeons."

25 Now there was a man in Jerusalem, whose name was Simeon, and this man was righteous and devout, looking for the consolation of Israel, and the Holy Spirit was upon him. 26 And it had been revealed to him by the Holy Spirit that he should not see death before he had seen the Lord's Christ. 27 And inspired by the Spirit he came into the temple; and when the parents brought in the child Jesus, to do for him according to the custom of the law, 28 he took him up in his arms and blessed God and said,

29 "Lord, now lettest thou thy servant
    depart in peace,
according to thy word;
30 for mine eyes have seen thy salvation
31 which thou hast prepared in the
    presence of all peoples,

32 a light for revelation to the Gentiles,
and for glory to thy people Israel."

33 And his father and his mother marveled at what was said about him; 34 and Simeon blessed them and said to Mary his mother,

"Behold, this child is set for the fall
    and rising of many in Israel, and for
a sign that is spoken against
35 (and a sword will pierce through
    your own soul also),
that thoughts out of many hearts may be
    revealed."

36 And there was a prophetess, Anna, the daughter of Phanuel, of the tribe of Asher; she was of a great age, having lived with her husband seven years from her virginity, 37 and as a widow till she was eighty-four. She did not depart from the temple, worshiping with fasting and prayer night and day. 38 And coming up at that very hour she gave thanks to God, and spoke of him to all who were looking for the redemption of Jerusalem.

39 And when they had performed everything according to the law of the Lord, they returned into Galilee, to their own city, Nazareth. 40 And the child grew and became strong, filled with wisdom; and the favor of God was upon him.

Reflecting on the Word

Mary and Joseph come to the temple, the center of Israel's faith, to carry out two Jewish customs: the mother's purification on the fortieth day after childbirth (Leviticus 12:1-8) and the consecration of the first-born son (Exodus 13:1-2, 11-16). Jesus' parents are observant Jews who greatly respect the Mosaic law and conscientiously fulfill its requirements (Luke 2:22, 23, 24, 27, 39).

During the time of Israel's slavery in Egypt, more than a millennium before the birth of Christ, the angel of death spared the first-born sons of the Hebrews while he slew all the first-born sons of the Egyptians (Exodus 12:12-13, 23, 29). Consequently, every first-born male Israelite was considered holy, that is, "set apart," and was dedicated to the Lord's service. Once the duties of offering worship and sacrifices on behalf of all the Israelites were reserved to the tribe of Levi (Numbers 3:5-13), first-born who did not belong to that tribe were exempted from performing these ritual services. However, to show that they continued to be God's special property, a rite of redemption was to be performed to free them from the requirement of serving all their lives in the temple as the consecrated of Yahweh: Mosaic law decreed that the Israelites offer a sacrifice as a symbolic form of ransom. Mary and Joseph fulfill this decree to "redeem" Jesus as they now bring him to the temple.

Consecrating Jesus in the temple, the site of Jewish ritual sacrifice, foreshadows the offering that Mary will repeatedly make of her son throughout her life by giving him over to God's will and plan. Many artists who have depicted the Presentation portray Mary holding the child out to Simeon over an altar, thus anticipating the redeeming sacrifice of Jesus' death on the cross: The "salvation" Simeon proclaims (Luke 2:30) will be accomplished by Christ's atoning sacrifice for our sins.

Simeon, like John the Baptist, stands as a link between the old covenant and the new. The eager longing of generations of devout Jews who awaited the Messiah begins to be satisfied as he takes the child Jesus in his arms: "For mine eyes have seen thy salvation . . . a light for revelation to the Gentiles, and for glory to thy people Israel" (Luke 2:30, 32).

God's assurance to Simeon that he would live long enough to see the Lord's Christ (Luke 2:26)—the "Anointed One"—must have heightened his expectancy and comforted him as he grew older. He studied the ancient prophecies to deepen his understanding of God's plan of salvation and, as a consequence, he was not daunted or disheartened by its paradoxes or incongruities. Nor is he caught unawares when Mary and Joseph bring their son to the temple to fulfill the law: Constantly alert and sensitive to the Holy Spirit, he is poised to welcome the child whom God points out to him through the Spirit's inspiration (2:27). Thus, while others expected a richly born warrior king, Simeon recognizes as savior the baby brought by a humble couple from Galilee. His long years of faithfulness and unflagging faith in the promise of God are rewarded as he holds the Messiah—the one sent not only to redeem Israel but the Gentiles as well (2:31-32).

Simeon prophesies that Mary's child will be accepted by some but rejected by many—a sign "spoken against," a sign through who hearts will be laid bare to God's scrutiny and judgment. With prophetic insight, the aged priest comprehends something of the mysterious mission and destiny of this child and warns the mother that she, too, will be pierced through with pain (Luke 2:34-35). As Pope John Paul II wrote of this encounter:

> Simeon's words seem like a second Annunciation to Mary, for they tell her of the actual historical situation in which the Son is to accomplish his mission, namely, in misunderstanding and sorrow. While this announcement on the one hand confirms her faith in the accomplishment of the divine promises of salvation, on the other hand it also reveals to her that she will have to live her obedience of faith in suffering, at the side of the suffering Savior, and that her motherhood will be mysterious and sorrowful. (*Redemptoris Mater*, 16)

Anna, too, has been prepared by her long vigil of prayer. Like a sentry at the post waiting through the night for the coming dawn, she keeps watch for the coming of the Messiah. Neither her vision nor her hope has been dimmed as she patiently remains on the lookout. Rather, it is her eagerness and readiness to catch sight of him that keeps her in tune with the Holy Spirit. When she finally sees the child in Simeon's arms, her gratitude cannot be contained but spills over. What joy to finally lay eyes on the one she had already spent her long life worshiping! Anna eagerly shares this joy, becoming one of God's first messengers to publicly proclaim the coming of the Lord to all who looked forward to his salvation (Luke 2:38).

Through the years that lie ahead, Mary and Joseph will marvel at what they have been told about their son as he grows in strength and wisdom, the favor of God upon him (Luke 2:33, 40).

Pondering the Word

1. What personal qualities and character traits of Mary and Joseph does the Presentation scene highlight? With what adjectives would you describe Mary and Joseph, based on the verses recording their behavior in the temple?

_____

_____

_____

_____

_____

_____

_____

_____

_____

2. Refer to Luke 2:25-28 for a biblical "portrait" of Simeon. How would you describe him in your own words? What does Luke's description of Anna (2:36-38) indicate about her character?

_____

_____

_____

_____

_____

_____

_____

_____

_____

3. List all the descriptive phrases and titles that Simeon applies to Jesus in his prophecies (Luke 2:30-32, 34-35). What do his words tell you about Jesus' mission? In what ways will Jesus become a sign "spoken against"? What does it mean to you that "thoughts out of many hearts" will be "revealed" by Jesus?

_____

_____

_____

_____

_____

_____

_____

_____

_____

4. What does Simeon's prophecy (Luke 2:35) indicate about Mary's role in God's plan of salvation? About her relationship to her son? Why do you think Simeon forewarned Mary that she would suffer?

_____

_____

_____

_____

_____

_____

_____

5. Mary and Joseph "marvel" at what Simeon told them about their child (Luke 2:33). What earlier verses from Luke's Gospel does this call to mind? What can you learn from these verses about Mary and Joseph's attitude toward the mysteries of God?

_____

_____

_____

_____

_____

_____

_____

_____

_____

6. Make note of each of the references to the Holy Spirit in Luke's account of the Presentation. What do the lives of Simeon and Anna indicate about the Spirit's action and role?

_____

_____

_____

_____

_____

_____

_____

_____

_____

_____

Living the Word

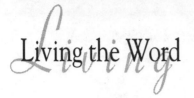

1. Do you ever find it difficult to obey God's commandments and the precepts of the church? If so, why? What can you learn from the example of Mary and Joseph obeying God's law?

_____

_____

_____

_____

_____

_____

_____

_____

2. Mary and Joseph made a humble offering of two turtledoves or pigeons when they came to the temple. What can you offer to God from your own life? Your time? A particular skill or talent?

_____

_____

_____

_____

_____

_____

_____

_____

3. Is there something in particular that you are currently waiting for God to do for you? If you have grown bored or complacent with waiting for God's word and promises to be fulfilled in your life, what can you do to renew your hope? What can you do to become a more patient person?

_____

_____

_____

_____

_____

_____

_____

_____

_____

4. When have you experienced a "prompting" of the Holy Spirit in your life? What happened when you obeyed and acted on this sense?

_____

_____

_____

_____

_____

_____

_____

_____

_____

5. Think of specific instances in your life when the Lord was made present to you through other people. How did you respond?

_____

_____

_____

_____

_____

_____

_____

_____

_____

_____

6. How often do you openly tell others—as Anna did—about God's salvation and about his goodness to you? If you are hesitant to do this, why? Express your gratitude for the ways you have experienced Jesus' salvation in your life in a prayer of praise to God.

_____

_____

_____

_____

_____

_____

_____

_____

_____

_____

Rooted in the Word

Mary: A Portrait of Surrender and Sacrifice

The Presentation is a harbinger of sufferings to come—the sufferings of both Jesus and Mary. This visit to the temple with its altar of sacrifice is a preface to Jesus' offering of his life on Calvary as well as a foreshadowing of the pain his mother would endure: "A sword will pierce through your own soul also" (Luke 2:35). There Mary silently repeats her *fiat* of the Annunciation, accepting God's will not only for her own life, but for the life of her son.

As Jesus' mother, Mary is intimately connected to his sacrifice. In presenting her infant son before God, she fulfills a kind of priestly role. Though her natural inclination was probably to shy away from pain to herself and, most especially, to protect her child from it, she will renew this offering many times throughout her life. Again and again she will release and surrender Jesus to God's purposes, enduring the grief of separation and of seeing him rejected, until she finally comes to stand at the foot of his cross.

Mary made the offering of her life to God—and she made the ultimate offering of a mother, letting go of her son as he surrendered himself to the Father, a sacrifice for our salvation.

Read and prayerfully reflect on these additional Scripture passages that portray Mary's and Jesus' attitude of surrender and the ways they offered themselves in sacrifice to God:

Mary said, "Behold, I am the handmaid of the Lord; let it be to me according to your word." (Luke 1:38)

Standing by the cross of Jesus were his mother, and his mother's sister, Mary the wife of Clopas, and Mary Magdalene. (John 19:25)

[Christ] entered once for all into the Holy Place, taking not the blood of goats and calves but his own blood, thus securing an eternal redemption. (Hebrews 9:12)

It is impossible that the blood of bulls and goats should take away sins. Consequently, when Christ came into the world, he said,

"Sacrifices and offerings thou hast
  not desired,
but a body hast thou prepared for me;
in burnt offerings and sin offerings
  thou hast taken no pleasure.

Then I said, 'Lo, I have come to do
thy will, O God,'
as it is written of me in the roll
of the book."
When he said the above, "Thou hast
neither desired nor taken pleasure in
sacrifices and offerings and burnt offerings and sin offerings" (these are offered
according to the law), then he added,
"Lo, I have come to do thy will." He
abolishes the first in order to establish
the second. And by that will we have
been sanctified through the offering of
the body of Jesus Christ once for all.
(Hebrews 10:4-10)

Abraham: Another Portrait of Surrender and Sacrifice

Read Genesis 22:1-14

Abraham's willing response, "Here am I," when God called to him (Genesis 22:1, 11) anticipates Mary's words: "Behold, I am the handmaid of the Lord; let it be to me according to your word" (Luke 1:38). The great patriarch whom St. Paul later called "our father in faith" (Romans 4:12) was ready to fulfill God's mysterious command: "Take your son, your only son Isaac whom you love, and go to the land of Moriah, and offer him there as a burnt offering" (Genesis 22:2). Jewish tradition identifies Mount Moriah with the site of the temple in Jerusalem (2 Chronicles 3:1)—where Mary, too, offered her son to God in the Presentation.

As he prepared to obediently sacrifice his son in recognition that the child belonged to God, Abraham surely knew the same deep anguish that Mary later would experience. Then God stayed the elderly father's hand (Genesis 22:12) and provided a lamb for the sacrifice instead (22:7-8, 13). Isaac, laid upon the wood on the altar (22:9), is a type of Christ, the Lamb of God, who was laid on the wood of the cross and sacrificed for our sins. Abraham, like Mary, surrendered his only son to God—and received Isaac back "as though he had been raised from the dead" (Hebrews 11:19). And God himself "did not spare his own Son, but gave him up for us all" (Romans 8:32), delivering him over to death and restoring him to life again for our salvation.

Treasuring the Word

A Reading from *In the Likeness of Christ* by Edward Leen, C.S. Sp.

The Presentation in the Temple

As Simeon's words penetrated to her consciousness . . . [Mary] at last grasped in all their significance those texts which set forth the history of a Messiah destined for pain and death. The Messiah is now her Son, and she realizes that her own child is to undergo, at the hands of His Own people, contradiction and trial and a rejection culminating in a cruel death. . . . "And Simeon said to Mary, His Mother, Behold this Child is set for the fall, and for the resurrection of many in Israel, and for a sign which will be contradicted." Her mother's heart was wrung with anguish as the sword of this bitter prophecy was plunged into it and as it turned in the deep wound it made. . . . She realized that it would be asked of her not merely to allow the Divine Will to pursue its course or merely submit to that Will in its dealings with Jesus, but also, over and above all that, to identify her will with that Will of God, and to make the voluntary sacrifice of the gift that had been placed in her arms. She was asked to will the sacrifice of Jesus. It was an incredibly hard thing to ask of a mother. It was much to ask her to accept— but to will it! That was something which would be demanded only of a sanctity like

Mary's. And her sanctity did not flinch before God's demand. And when her will surrendered, a depth of calm and peace possessed her soul, that wonderful peace and calm that always follows on a sacrifice generously made for God. . . .

This Mystery of the Presentation, although of such tragic intensity, is not without some light that relieves the gloom. . . . In the joy that irradiated the souls of the prophet Simeon and the prophetess Anna, Mary had a glimpse of the glory and gladness that, to men of good will, would be brought by the coming of her Son. In them she saw all those for whom He would not be a sign to be contradicted but a sign to be followed with loyalty and enthusiasm. In these two holy souls Mary saw verified the conditions which prepare the way for the discovery of God on earth. Anna, after the few years of her happy married life had sped by . . . spent long years in mortification of the flesh and in prayer. The result was that her soul responded instinctively to the presence of God. She recognized who the child was and its mother and she spoke of Him "to all that looked for the redemption of Israel."

Simeon, like Anna, had passed his life in self-denial and in the study of divine things. His self-denial took the form of detachment and aloofness with regard to merely earthly interests. Earth had lost its grip on him. He swung free from its attractions. Valuing nothing but God, death had no terrors for him: because for him it would not mean a sundering or a snapping of ties. He wanted only one thing on earth and that was to behold with his eyes the promised redeemer. Completely detached from, and therefore soaring above earthly things, his eyes were able to discern clearly the vision he longed for when at last it presented itself to him. To the perfectly detached there is given an unblurred and undimmed vision of spiritual realities. Our vision is faulty because we wish to fix, with our regard, other things along with God. Simeon was heard beyond his desires. It was given him on earth not only to see Jesus; he was allowed to hold Jesus in his arms. At the contact his soul overflowed with peace and happiness and earth and all it contained lost all significance in his eyes, and he could say: "Now Thou dost dismiss Thy servant, O Lord, according to Thy word, in peace."

We, too, may look for the great grace that was granted Simeon. He has shown us how to prepare for and merit it. The desire of our hearts should be to see Jesus. There is only one path that will lead us to the vision. It is the way of detachment and of prayer.

Pray to Mary "Queen of Peace" for peace in your life.

"Indulgence"
↓
"time off purgatory"

To my girls— Pray for God's guidance in marriage.

The Adoration of the Magi

When [the wise men] saw the star, they rejoiced exceedingly with great joy; and going into the house they saw the child with Mary his mother, and they fell down and worshiped him.
Matthew 2:10-11

The Magi gaze in deep wonder at what they see: heaven on earth, earth in heaven, man in God, God in man, one whom the whole universe cannot contain now enclosed in a tiny body. As they look, they believe and do not question, as their symbolic gifts bear witness: incense for God, gold for a king, myrrh for one who is to die.
St. Peter Chrysologus,
Sermon 160

Journey by Starlight

A star rises in the silence of the night
and shatters the deep darkness of my heart's
loneliness and longing.

A star breaks away from the lowly horizon
and climbs into the heights
where its brightness sings forth in glory and in hope.

A star's shining song wakes the dawn
and my dull and sleeping spirit
and fills my blind eyes
with new light.

Set out upon the way, my soul, set out upon the way.
A Savior has been born for you.
Make haste and go and find him.

The journeying is long.
The way lies through wasted desert land,
yet grace is in the very seeking.
With each step the star's light
burns deeper into my heart
and fills me with its searing brightness
till all of me is aglow with its fire.

With each step my burdens and my poor, shoddy riches
are laid down by the wayside
as I press on toward the new life awaiting me
and approach with heart and hands
open wide to its embrace.

Yes, grace lies upon the edges of this long journey,
and time to prepare the heart.

The star leads onward to the Truth,
clothed not in the guise of kingly might and splendor
but in the frail, naked flesh of a newborn babe
wrapped in swaddling bands and lying in a manger
where God shares our poverty and weakness,
made like us in all but sin.

Look deeper as the star's light shines upon this Truth
and dispels the gloomy darkness.

Sink down and kneel.
Bow low before his presence there upon the hay.

Lay down your crown, O soul, alongside the wise men's there.
Lay down your pomp and power,
your privileges and pride and presumptions,
your own rights and righteousness.

Offer there your treasures at the manger:
Desire and dream purified to finest gold,
hopes and prayers raised and sacrificed
as fragrant frankincense,
griefs and pains and disappointments anointed
and laid to rest with myrrh's balm.

Let the Child take these poor treasures in hand
to make of them his playthings,
there to see the pleasure he takes in them,
there to await what he will make of them for you,
far better than your own doing.

And having offered my heart's gifts
and done him homage in silent adoration,
now I return to my own land.
But the star's light is my companion
and burns steadily within,
warming my stony coldness,
enlightening my vision,
and guiding my steps along the pilgrim's way
till I meet this Child again,
then throned and robed in full majesty and royal splendor
at his Father's side.

Matthew 2:1-12

2:1 Now when Jesus was born in Bethlehem of Judea in the days of Herod the king, behold, wise men from the East came to Jerusalem, saying, 2 "Where is he who has been born king of the Jews? For we have seen his star in the East, and have come to worship him." 3 When Herod the king heard this, he was troubled, and all Jerusalem with him; 4 and assembling all the chief priests and scribes of the people, he inquired of them where the Christ was to be born. 5 They told him, "In Bethlehem of Judea; for so it is written by the prophet:

> 6 'And you, O Bethlehem, in the land
> of Judah,
> are by no means least among the
> rulers of Judah;
> for from you shall come a ruler
> who will govern my people Israel.'"

7 Then Herod summoned the wise men secretly and ascertained from them what time the star appeared; 8 and he sent them to Bethlehem, saying, "Go and search diligently for the child, and when you have found him bring me word, that I too may come and worship him." 9 When they had heard the king they went their way; and lo, the star which they had seen in the East went before them, till it came to rest over the place where the child was. 10 When they saw the star, they rejoiced exceedingly with great joy; 11 and going into the house they saw the child with Mary his mother, and they fell down and worshiped him. Then, opening their treasures, they offered him gifts, gold and frankincense and myrrh. 12 And being warned in a dream not to return to Herod, they departed to their own country by another way.

Reflecting on the Word

Magi were learned sages from the East. The word *magoi*, meaning "wise men," was the Greek form of the Old Persian *magav*. Perhaps Persian astrologers of a priestly caste, Matthew's wise men are the first to seek an encounter with Jesus. Prompted by the sight of an extraordinary star that they recognize as the portent of a newborn king of the Jews, they undertake an arduous journey to find and honor him (Matthew 2:2). Since they were not Jewish, the wise men can be considered the first Gentiles to receive the call to salvation in Christ.

The visit of the Magi belongs to the earliest documented Christian traditions—the scene of their adoration is already depicted at the beginning of the second century on the walls of the catacombs in Rome. Christian imagination, drawing on Isaiah 60:1-6 and Psalm 72:10-11, 15, later viewed them as "kings." This imaginativeness even gave them names and associated them with various ages and virtues: Caspar, a young man representing the dawn and innocence, full of faith; Balthazar, with the maturity of middle age, in the noontime of life, full of hope; and Melchior, aging with the setting sun, full of years and charity.

Thirsting for truth, the wise men willingly make this long journey in search of it. As the art historian Sr. Wendy Beckett notes:

This is a story of incredible perseverance, earnestness, and the rewards that follow.

The good news came easily to the shepherds; it caused many difficulties for these distant scholars, who made great sacrifices of time and energy, all to track down a possibility. Remote in their eastern lands, they would never have heard of Christ, but they studied, they worried, and they pondered on the meaning of the star. They took active steps to solve the mystery, and they found what they sought. (*Sister Wendy's Nativity*)

In contrast to these foreign seekers, the Jews' own king is greatly disturbed by the thought of the birth of a royal child—a threat to his throne (Matthew 2:3). An Edomite of non-Jewish background, Herod had been appointed "King of the Jews" by the Roman Senate in 40 B. C. to replace the collapsing dynasty of Jewish priestly rulers. The prospect of the fulfillment of the ancient messianic prophecy troubles Herod, because it also foretold disaster for his family: "A star shall come forth from Jacob, and a scepter shall rise out of Israel; . . . Edom shall be dispossessed" (Numbers 24:17-18).

After first seeking the kingly heir in Jerusalem, the Magi are directed to Bethlehem (Matthew 2:5-6; Micah 5:2). The star wondrously guides them to the house where Mary and Joseph are staying with their infant son (Matthew 2:9-11). What a different scene meets their eyes there: in place of the riches of Herod's palace, the homey simplicity of this poor family's dwelling; not the power and guilty subterfuges of Herod but the weakness and innocence of a newborn baby. But the wise men are not as concerned about outward appearance as with the mysteries of faith. Looking beyond these unexpected circumstances, they recognize him whom they long sought, and fall down and humbly worship the child (2:11). Worship is the only fitting response to the presence and revelation of God. They neither ask anything of the child nor expect anything in return. Their act of adoration is satisfaction and reward enough for them when they reach their goal.

The Magi honor the child with costly gifts that symbolically reveal something of his nature and destiny to us: gold, the attribute of a king; frankincense, burnt in temples throughout the ancient world and an allusion to divinity; and myrrh, used in anointing the dead for burial and signifying that this child has been born in order to die (Matthew 2:11). Bringing more than gifts, the visitors offer their homage and faith—a prophetic sign of the Gentiles' recognition of Jesus as the Messiah and of the universality of God's plan of salvation.

How Mary must marvel at the strange company her baby again draws to himself! We can only imagine Mary and Joseph's awe and amazement as this exotic caravan appears at their door. Although no words pass between the Magi and the baby, we might wonder about the conversations they held with Mary and Joseph. Did Mary tell them about the message of the heavenly host of angels and the visit of the shepherds? And did these foreign kings recognize the regal role of the young woman and accord her honor, in Eastern fashion, as "queen mother"? In works of art, Mary is often depicted with the Christ Child on her lap, her own figure forming a sort of throne for him, evoking an image of queenship.

Although Matthew does not mention Joseph, most likely he is present too. It would have been unusual and even improper in that society for Mary to receive foreign visitors alone. Moreover, Middle Eastern hospitality demands that the hosts care for their guests graciously, a responsibility Joseph would have assumed. The entourage, tired and weary from their long journey, might even have stayed several days.

Finally, the Magi return home "another way" (Mathew 2:12). Finding Christ indeed leads to living "another way," the new way of God's kingdom. Surely these wise men followed this new path the rest of their lives— lives now filled with greater faith, joy, hope, and peace.

Pondering the Word

1. The scene Matthew paints of the wise men's visit is rich in prophetic overtones. Read Numbers 24:17-18 and Micah 5:2. What do these prophecies indicate to you about the Messiah? In what ways do you see them fulfilled in Matthew's account of this visit?

_____

_____

_____

_____

_____

_____

_____

_____

2. What personal traits and qualities would you attribute to the wise men? Base your observations on what Matthew recounts about their actions. What was their primary motivation in following the star? List the reasons why their quest required great faith.

_____

_____

_____

_____

_____

_____

_____

_____

3. What impression do you get of King Herod from this portion of Matthew's account? (In your considerations, don't jump ahead yet to Herod's future actions.)

_____

_____

_____

_____

_____

_____

_____

_____

_____

4. What additional knowledge about their child does the Magi's visit bring to Mary and Joseph? What mixture of emotions do you think the visit inspired in them?

_____

_____

_____

_____

_____

_____

_____

_____

_____

5. The solemnity of the Epiphany commemorates the first manifestation of the Son of God to the pagan world. In the first centuries of the Eastern church, it was known as the "Theophany" or the "Feast of the Illumination." The Epiphany was made a universal feast of the church in the fourth century. Why do you think the church uses Isaiah 60:1-6 as the first reading in the liturgy of the Epiphany? What response does this prophecy evoke in you?

_____

_____

_____

_____

_____

_____

_____

_____

_____

_____

Living the Word
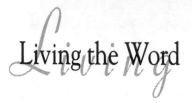

1. The Magi discovered the Messiah in an unexpected place and setting. Can you think of a time when you encountered the presence of Jesus in an unlikely situation or place? How can you better recognize Jesus in the day-to-day events of your life?

_____

_____

_____

_____

_____

_____

_____

_____

2. The Magi were seekers and risk-takers. What does this say to you? Is there any area in your life right now in which you are feeling complacent or spiritually lethargic? What is one action you can take to overcome this feeling?

_____

_____

_____

_____

_____

_____

_____

_____

3. What would you call a "guiding star" in your life? Have you been "sidetracked" in any way from seeking Christ?

_____

_____

_____

_____

_____

_____

_____

_____

4. The wise men were pilgrims whose faith flourished as it found support in the fellowship of friends also seeking the light. How do your friends help you move toward Christ?

_____

_____

_____

_____

_____

_____

_____

_____

5. To adore Jesus was the sole purpose of the Magi's journey. Toward what goal in life do you direct all your energies?

_____

_____

_____

_____

_____

_____

_____

_____

6. Has God ever used a visitor or guest to communicate something of himself to you? If so, why do you think he used that means?

_____

_____

_____

_____

_____

_____

_____

_____

Rooted in the Word

Mary: A Portrait of Adoration

An angelic choir glorified God on the night of the Savior's birth, and later the Magi came from afar to bow and kneel before him in homage. As Mary held her child in her arms for the visitors to see, surely it was with profound reverence and awe. As she looked lovingly upon him, she knew that she was holding close to her breast the "Son of the Most High" (Luke 1:32). God himself had entrusted his own Son to her care. In describing Mary's contemplation of Christ, Pope John Paul II wrote, "Mary's gaze, ever filled with adoration and wonder, would never leave him" (*Rosarium Virginis Mariae*, 10).

With Mary and the wise men, we too are privileged to gaze upon Jesus, to behold his glory (John 1:14) and to contemplate him in a spirit of loving adoration. And as we fix our eyes and our hearts on him, we are transformed, through love, into the likeness of Jesus himself.

Read and prayerfully reflect on these additional Scripture passages that describe gazing upon God in a spirit of contemplative adoration:

One thing have I asked of the LORD,
    that will I seek after;
that I may dwell in the house of the LORD
    all the days of my life,
to behold the beauty of the LORD,
    and to inquire in his temple.
(Psalm 27:4)

My soul thirsts for God,
    for the living God.
When shall I come and behold
    the face of God? (Psalm 42:2)

The Word became flesh and dwelt among us, full of grace and truth; and we have beheld his glory, glory as of the only Son from the Father. (John 1:14)

We all, with unveiled face, beholding the glory of the Lord, are being changed into his likeness, from one degree of glory to another. (2 Corinthians 3:18)

The throne of God and of the Lamb shall be in [the new Jerusalem, the city of God], and his servants shall worship him; they shall see his face. (Revelation 22:3-4)

Mary of Bethany: Another Portrait of Adoration

Read Mark 14:3-9

Like the Magi, Mary of Bethany spent herself on Jesus in a generous act of love and adoration. With no thought of what others would think of her or of the cost to herself, she lovingly gave to Jesus the best of what she had—her heart's devotion as well as a precious gift of ointment.

Mary kept none of the expensive perfume for her own use, but lavishly anointed her Master with it (Mark 14:3). When others complained of such "waste" (14:4), Jesus defended and praised his dear friend Mary, saying, "She has done a beautiful thing to me" (14:6).

At Jesus' birth, the wise men adored the infant by offering him gifts fit for a king, among them myrrh, a foreshadowing of his death. Later, Mary of Bethany expressed her love and homage by anointing Jesus' body "beforehand" with pure nard to prepare him for burial (Mark 14:8). After Jesus' death, Nicodemus will bring a mixture of myrrh and aloes to wrap with his body in the linen shroud, a final act of reverence to his crucified Lord as he was laid to rest in the tomb (John 19:39-40).

Treasuring the Word

A Reading from an Epiphany Sermon by St. Bernard of Clairvaux

The Manifestation to the Magi

Whatever are you doing, you Magi? You worship a baby at the breast, in a poor shed, in common swaddling clothes! Is he then *God*? God is in his holy temple, surely (Psalm 11:4); the Lord's seat is in heaven; yet you are looking for him in a wretched stable and on his mother's lap! What do you mean by offering him gold? Is he a king? If so, where is his palace, where his throne, and where the many members of a royal court? Is the stable a palace? Is the manger a throne? Do Joseph and Mary constitute a court? How have wise men become such fools as to adore a child, whose age and whose relations' poverty alike deserve contempt?

They have become fools, that they may be wise. The Spirit has taught them in advance what later the apostle preached, "Let him who would be wise become as a fool, that so he may be wise. For because through wisdom the world in its wisdom could not have knowledge of God, it pleased God by the foolishness of preaching to save them that believe" (1 Corinthians 1:21). Might we not well have been afraid, my brethren, lest seeing such unworthy sights should be a stumbling block to those wise men, and make them think that they had been deceived?

From the royal city, where they reckoned the king should be sought, they are directed to Bethlehem, an insignificant village; they enter a stable, and find a tiny infant wrapped in swaddling clothes. But the stable does not seem mean to them, they find no cause of stumbling in the swaddling bands, nor does the suckling's speechlessness offend them. They fall on their faces, they revere him as King, they worship him as God. Of a truth he, who led them hither, has instructed them too; he, who urged them on by means of the star without, has himself taught them in their inmost heart. Wherefore this manifestation of the Lord has glorified this day, and the sages' faithful act of worship rendered it a day to be observed with reverence and love. . . .

I beseech you to behold and see how keen of sight is faith, and to consider carefully what lynx eyes it has. It knows the Son of God in a sucking babe, it knows him hanging on a cross, it knows him as he dies; for the Magi knew him in the stable, wrapped in swaddling bands; the thief recognized him on the cross, pierced with nails; and the centurion acknowledged Life in death. The two former saw the power of God in extreme bodily weakness; the last-named saw the Highest Spirit in the yielding of his breath (John 19:30). The Magi see the

Word of God in wordless babyhood, and confess by their gifts the faith that the others express in words. The thief proclaims him King, and the centurion says that he is both man and the Son of God—exactly what the Magi's own three gifts declare, save that their incense shows him to be God, rather than Son of God.

The Flight into Egypt

And [Joseph] rose and took the child and his mother by night, and departed to Egypt.
Matthew 2:14

The mystery of the innocents is that they are the victims. The divine eagle gathered them as booty to himself. The blow aimed by the tyrant at our Lord fell on them instead. They serve as a kind of guard of honor to the divine Child—and the militant dialogue between God and anti-god in which they are caught up earns them heaven.
Alfred Delp, S.J.,
The Prison Meditations of
Father Alfred Delp

Freed from the Fowler's Snare

Too soon Simeon's words found their mark
and Mary's heart was sharply pierced with pain.

Driven out into the dark by the angel's warning,
the young family slipped away from Bethlehem,
hearts beating in agonizing haste.
No safety for them now in David's city
as Herod stretched forth his oft-bloodied hands once again,
this time to slay in sullen jealousy
the blameless sons of David's line.
(How pitiable that he should fear as rivals to his might and power
nurslings at their mothers' breasts!)

Mary wrapped the sleeping child tightly in her cloak
and held him close,
protecting him from the cold shadows of night
(and hovering sword)
and muffling any drowsy whimper that might reveal his presence
and draw death's horsemen closer on their heels.
Might she then have heard behind her
terrified cries rise in an infant chorus of agony
and suddenly fall horrifyingly silent?
Perhaps she had sat that morning with Bethlehem's young mothers,
smiling in maternal contentment
as they watched their babies playing at their feet,
the sun warm and comfortable upon their innocence.
And now, in that harrowing darkness,
did Mary and Joseph press on in alarm
while the plaintive wailing of these women stabbed their souls?
Were the sounds of grief etched on her heart that night,
never to be erased?

Through the long years ahead,
did the virgin mother often weep her own silent tears
for Rachel's children who were no more
(and for her companions of those sunny days
who had too early lost their freshness and the joys of motherhood)?
Did she often see in her mind's eye the tombs
hewn in Judea's stony hills 'round Bethlehem
and filled with the first (of millions)
to be martyred for her son's sake—
and mourn those bright-eyed boys who had never enjoyed their manhood?

When they reached Egypt's sheltering safety,
perhaps the tired couple prayed together
(in voices trembling with relief)
their father David's psalm of thanks:
Blessed be the LORD,
who has not given us as prey to their teeth!
We have escaped as a bird from the snare of the fowlers;
the snare is broken, and we have escaped!

Did Mary then ponder in her heart the mysterious ways of God,
suspecting that her child had been spared
(and at what price!)
only that he should battle with death at the hour of his own choosing?
Deeper sorrows lay ahead—that she knew with certainty—
since all Simeon's austere words were not yet fulfilled.

How unsearchable are his judgments
and how inscrutable his ways!
For who has known the mind of the Lord,
or who has been his counselor?

Immortal now, these Holy Innocents
have a place around God's throne
(perhaps playing at his footstool)
and the Mighty One himself
pays glad gratitude to them for once saving
with their tiny bodies
the incarnate life of his own Son.

There Mary, too, smiles upon them
and offers them a mother's thanks.

2:13 Now when they had departed, behold, an angel of the Lord appeared to Joseph in a dream and said, "Rise, take the child and his mother, and flee to Egypt, and remain there till I tell you; for Herod is about to search for the child, to destroy him." 14 And he rose and took the child and his mother by night, and departed to Egypt, 15 and remained there until the death of Herod. This was to fulfill what the Lord had spoken by the prophet, "Out of Egypt have I called my son."

16 Then Herod, when he saw that he had been tricked by the wise men, was in a furious rage, and he sent and killed all the male children in Bethlehem and in all that region who were two years old or under, according to the time which he had ascertained from the wise men. 17 Then was fulfilled what was spoken by the prophet Jeremiah:

18 "A voice was heard in Ramah,
wailing and loud lamentation,
Rachel weeping for her children;
she refused to be consoled,
because they were no more."

19 But when Herod died, behold, an angel of the Lord appeared in a dream to Joseph in Egypt, saying, 20 "Rise, take the child and his mother, and go to the land of Israel, for those who sought the child's life are dead." 21 And he rose and took the child and his mother, and went to the land of Israel. 22 But when he heard that Archelaus reigned over Judea in place of his father Herod, he was afraid to go there, and being warned in a dream he withdrew to the district of Galilee. 23 And he went and dwelt in a city called Nazareth, that what was spoken by the prophets might be fulfilled, "He shall be called a Nazarene."

Reflecting on the Word

In this unsettling story, Joseph and Mary must go a way that is not of their own choosing. Nonetheless, it is the *right* way, a way directed by God to rescue their child from danger.

Joseph, again visited by an angel as he dreams, is warned to take his family and flee to protect the baby from Herod's murderous intent. Many times already Egypt had been a place of refuge for God's people (Genesis 12:10; 46:4; 1 Kings 11:40; Jeremiah 26:21). Now, at God's command, the frightened family heads into this foreign land—perhaps to the city of Alexandria, where there was a large Jewish colony—and into an uncertain future, leaving behind all that was familiar and dear to them.

Willing obedience and unquestioning service are the secrets of Joseph's life. Although he speaks no word, they are the clear message he leaves us. Mary trusts in her husband's care, and silently follows him into exile. How quickly Simeon's words have come to pass that Mary would be pierced by sorrows!

Any new parents can empathize with the plight of the holy family. Instead of taking delight in the home they had lovingly prepared for their baby, Joseph and Mary take to the road, departing by night in fear for the life of their child. This family in distress could well be invoked as the patron of those millions of refugees in misery who flee political oppression, ethnic genocide, war, or famine. Before he ever had a real home or knew a homeland, God-on-earth becomes a homeless, displaced person.

Herod the Great brought culture, prosperity, and magnificence to Judea with his enthusiasm for constructing great cities and fortresses. He even refurbished the temple in Jerusalem. Nonetheless, his thirty-three-year reign was one of terror. He executed anyone he suspected of being a threat to his power, including his own family members (one of his wives and two sons, according to the Jewish historian Josephus). Almost seventy years old at the time of Christ's birth, Herod was not ready to give up his kingship. It was a small matter to him to kill a few infants in a "preemptive strike" to protect his throne.

Imagine what pain Mary carried with her to Egypt—and throughout her whole life—knowing that innocent children suffered martyrdom because of her son.

Matthew links the sorrow of the mothers in Bethlehem to the grief experienced by Rachel, as described by the prophet Jeremiah. As the wife of the patriarch Jacob, Rachel wept for her "children," the tribes of Israel who were taken into exile in Babylon (Jeremiah 31:15; Matthew 2:18). Jewish tradition locates Rachel's tomb either on the outskirts of Bethlehem, where she gave birth to Benjamin and died (Genesis 35:16-20), or near Ramah, in the territory of Benjamin, (1 Samuel 10:2), a region that knew repeated devastation and sorrow in Israel's history (Isaiah 10:29; Hosea 5:8).

In the face of such horrendously evil deeds as King Herod's, we can only trust in God and take comfort in his promises: "God himself will be with [us]; he will wipe away every tear from [our] eyes, and death shall be no more, neither shall there be mourning nor crying nor pain any more" (Revelation 21:3-4).

"There is anguish for us, twenty centuries later, in thinking of the slain babies and their parents," according to Catholic apologist Frank Sheed, who wrote:

> For the babies the agony was soon over; in the next world they would come to know whom they had died to save and for all eternity would have that glory. For the parents, the pain would have lasted longer; but at death they too must have found that there was a special sense in which God was in their debt, as he had never been indebted to any. They and their children were the only ones who ever agonized in order to save God's life. (*To Know Christ Jesus*)

All the stopovers on the Messiah's itinerary that Matthew mentions in this account were planned and guided by the will of God. Born in Bethlehem to fulfill the prophecy of Micah (5:2), Jesus spends the next phase of his life in Egypt. In this, we recall the events of the Exodus, when another cruel king—the Egyptian Pharaoh—ordered the execution of all newborn Israelite males. Moses was saved by God's providence (Exodus 1:8-16, 22) and later led his people out of Egypt. Now Jesus, spared too by God's protection, will come as the "new Moses" to bring spiritual deliverance to God's people. By quoting the text, "Out of Egypt I called my son" (Hosea 11:1), Matthew identifies Jesus as God's Son and also suggests that Jesus is the personification of the people of God. Just as God called Israel out of Egypt in order to create a special people for himself, so he called Jesus out of Egypt into the land of Israel in order to create a new people.

Finally, Jesus returns to Nazareth in a now familiar pattern—at the angel's word to Joseph in a dream. Another prophecy about the Messiah's origins and identity is then fulfilled: "He shall be called a Nazorean." Pope John Paul II reflects on the quiet years ahead in his encyclical *Redemptoris Mater*:

> When the Holy Family returns to Nazareth after Herod's death, there begins the long *period of the hidden life*. She "who believed that there would be a fulfillment of what was spoken to her from the Lord" (Luke 1:45) lives the reality of these words day by day. And daily at her side is the Son to whom "*she gave the name Jesus*" . . .

> During the years of Jesus' hidden life in the house at Nazareth, *Mary's life* too is "*hid with Christ in God*" (Colossians 3:3) *through faith*. For faith is contact

with the mystery of God. Every day Mary is in constant contact with the ineffable mystery of God made man. (17)

The flight into Egypt and return to Nazareth give us an image of the lives of Mary and Joseph and their child as a journey of faith, with hearts set on God, "on the way" with his promises. As we so often experience ourselves, it is sometimes a difficult and challenging journey, but one with a sure Guide as our companion.

Pondering the Word

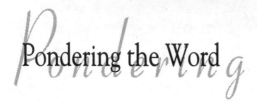

1. What character traits are exemplified by Joseph's response to the angel's directions? In what other events did he reveal these traits? How?

_____

_____

_____

_____

_____

_____

_____

_____

_____

_____

2. What does this episode tell you about Mary and Joseph's marriage relationship? What does it add to the impressions you formed of Mary in the previous events?

_____

_____

_____

_____

_____

_____

_____

_____

_____

_____

3. Reflect on the hardships Mary faced during her flight and exile in Egypt. What qualities do you think she displayed during this time?

_____

_____

_____

_____

_____

_____

_____

_____

_____

4. What desires and emotions were driving forces in Herod's life? What understanding of evil have you gained from this story?

_____

_____

_____

_____

_____

_____

_____

_____

_____

_____

5. Matthew often applies Old Testament prophecies to Jesus and notes their fulfillment in him. (See Matthew 1:23; 2:6, 15, 18, 23; Isaiah 7:14; Micah 5:2; and Jeremiah 31:15.) What significance do you think these prophecies had for Matthew's earliest readers, a largely Jewish audience? Why is their fulfillment significant for us today?

_____

_____

_____

_____

_____

_____

_____

_____

_____

6. Note as many indications of God's faithfulness as you can in Matthew's telling of these troubling events. What other aspects of God's nature and character does this story reveal?

_____

_____

_____

_____

_____

_____

_____

_____

_____

Living the Word

1. God used the Magi as part of his plan to reveal his salvation to the world. On the other hand, Herod tried to thwart God's plan. In what ways do you foster or hinder God's plan for your life? For the building of his kingdom?

_____

_____

_____

_____

_____

_____

_____

_____

2. Herod was the perpetrator of many evil deeds. What evil forces do you recognize at work in the world today? How can you protect yourself and others against evil forces and influences as Joseph protected his family?

_____

_____

_____

_____

_____

_____

_____

_____

3. How have you experienced God leading you on a "different but better path" than you would have chosen on your own? In what ways is your life a "journey of faith"? How do you see God guiding the course of your life?

_____

_____

_____

_____

_____

_____

_____

_____

_____

4. What does Joseph's prompt obedience and trust in God teach you? Have you ever taken an important step in your life "on short notice" or in "blind faith"? If so, what happened?

_____

_____

_____

_____

_____

_____

_____

_____

_____

5. Mary's implicit trust of Joseph allowed her to accept his decision to flee to Egypt. If you are married, was there ever a time when you had to trust your spouse with a decision that you didn't fully understand at the time? How can Mary's example help you to deepen your trust in God? In your spouse?

_____

_____

_____

_____

_____

_____

_____

_____

6. What is your attitude toward refugees and foreign immigrants? How can you offer help to the homeless?

_____

_____

_____

_____

_____

_____

_____

_____

Rooted in the Word

Mary: A Portrait of Steadfastness in Difficult Times

Mary was familiar with sorrow; her soul was steeped in it. "The modern woman," Pope Paul VI noted, "will recognize in Mary . . . a woman of strength who experienced poverty and suffering, flight and exile" (*Marialis Cultus*, 37). She must have grieved deeply that her infant son was so soon the target of hatred and that others died to protect his life. How, in the face of such heartrending pain and unfathomable evil, did she remain steadfast and unwavering in faith?

Though God's ways often seem incomprehensible and impenetrable, his love is sure and true, worthy of all trust. Mary was securely rooted in her knowledge of this love. She believed in God's love, leaned with her whole weight on it, relied on it—and so found strength and comfort in it to sustain her in difficult times.

We, too, are asked to "know and believe the love God has for us" (1 John 4:16). Like Mary, the more deeply we strike our roots in the soil of God's love, the more firmly we will stand when we encounter difficulties, trials, sorrows, or evil.

Read and prayerfully reflect on these additional Scripture passages to help keep in mind our source of strength in trial and the grace of God's comfort:

This I call to mind and therefore I have hope: The steadfast love of the LORD never ceases, his mercies never come to an end; they are new every morning; great is thy faithfulness. . . . For the Lord will not cast off for ever, but, though he cause grief, he will have compassion according to the abundance of his steadfast love; for he does not willingly afflict or grieve the sons of men. (Lamentations 3:21-23; 31-33)

We rejoice in our sufferings, knowing that suffering produces endurance, and endurance produces character, and character produces hope, and hope does not disappoint us, because God's love has been poured into our hearts through the Holy Spirit who has been given to us. (Romans 5:3-5)

Blessed be the God and Father of our Lord Jesus Christ, the Father of mercies and God of all comfort, who comforts us in all our affliction, so that we may be able to comfort those who are in any affliction, with the comfort with which we ourselves are comforted by God. For as we share abundantly in Christ's sufferings, so through Christ we share abundantly in comfort too. (2 Corinthians 1:3-5)

Be sober, be watchful. Your adversary the devil prowls around like a roaring lion, seeking some one to devour. Resist him, firm in your faith, knowing that the same experience of suffering is required of your brotherhood throughout the world. And after you have suffered a little while, the God of all grace, who has called you to his eternal glory in Christ, will himself restore, establish, and strengthen you. (1 Peter 5:8-10)

Naomi and Ruth:
Two Other Portraits of Steadfastness in Difficult Times

Read Ruth 1–2; 4:9-18

Naomi had, like Mary, departed from Bethlehem in a time of hardship, lived with her family in a land far from her own people, and known sorrow in outliving her husband and sons (Ruth 1:2-4). Her daughter-in-law Ruth knew similar sorrows. In spite of the great cost to herself, Ruth accompanied her mother-in-law back to Bethlehem, embracing Naomi's people and her God (1:16).

In her pain, Naomi bitterly attributed her sufferings to God's will (Ruth 1:20-21). Yet still she clung fast to the Lord, recognizing in Boaz's goodness that God was caring for her and Ruth. Thus, Naomi praised God, "whose kindness has not forsaken the living or the dead" (2:20). And Ruth's steadfastness eventually bore great fruit: God moved Boaz to take her as his wife and blessed her in childbirth. Ruth and Boaz's son, Obed, was the grandfather of David.

God filled the emptiness of Naomi and Ruth with the fullness of new life and turned their grief into joy. In Obed, Naomi was given an heir, a "restorer of life" (Ruth 4:15) to her. Her steadfastness did not go unrewarded by the God in whose loving care she placed all her hope. Ruth, as the great-grandmother of David, gained a place in the royal lineage of the Messiah and the honor of being among the forebears of Christ (Matthew 1:5).

Treasuring the Word

A Reading from *The Silence of Mary* by Ignacio Larrañaga, O.F.M. Cap.

The Fugitive Mother

Then, one day, the Lord spoke: "Rise, take the child and his mother, flee to Egypt, and stay there until I tell you" (Matthew 2:13). These few words brought a flood of questions to Mary's heart.

"Why is Herod searching for this Child? How did he find out about his birth? What wrong has he committed? Why does the king want to get rid of him? Flee to Egypt? Why not Samaria, Syria or Lebanon where Herod does not rule? How are we to survive there? What language will we speak? In which temple shall we worship? How long will we have to stay there? How long before God will tell us otherwise? Are the persecutors close?"

Again the terrible silence of God fell upon the young Mother like a dark cloud. How many times the same thing happens in our own lives. Suddenly, everything seems absurd. Nothing makes sense. Everything seems a blind and sinister fate. We feel like mere playthings in the midst of a whirlwind. God? If he exists and is all powerful, why does he permit all this? Why is he silent? We feel like rebelling, denying the whole thing.

Mary does not rebel, she abandons herself. To every problem she answers her "May it be done." A servant does not ask questions, she surrenders. "My Lord, I abandon myself in silence into your hands. Do with me what you will. I am ready for anything. I accept everything. I shall fight with every fiber of my being for the safety of the Child and for my own life. But during the struggle and after I will place my destiny in your hands." Thus Mary, in silence and peace, undertakes the flight into a strange land.

At this moment Mary entered into the condition of a political fugitive. The existence of this Child threatened the security of a throne. And the king, for his own security, threatened the life of the Child, who had to flee in the arms of his Mother to guarantee his survival.

To know Mary's state of mind during this escape, we must understand the psychology of a political fugitive. A political fugitive lives from one fright to another. He cannot sleep in the same place two successive nights. Every unfamiliar person is a potential informer. Any suspect is a police officer in civilian clothes. A fugitive lives dangerously, always on the defensive.

Thus Mary lived during that time, from one fright to another: "Those people behind us, would they be Herod's agents? Those coming toward us? Who are these people ahead of us? Those who have stopped just now? Should we sleep here tonight? What is better, to travel by day or by night?"

Another element of the flight—one realized in the psychology of every fugitive—was the need to move slowly yet in haste. Slowly because they could not travel by the main roads where they might be spotted by Herod's men; rather, they had to wind their way around the hills and secondary roads, through Hebron, Beersheba and Idumea. And in haste so as to leave Herod's kingdom as soon as possible and cross the border of El-Arish. . . .

In the midst of this barren, devastating solitude, surrounded by the most impressive silence of God, the fugitive Mother journeys, a heartrending figure, yet with the air of a great lady, humble, abandoned to the hands of the Father, full of an unshakable gentleness, repeating unceasingly her "Amen" while trying not to be discovered by the police.

The Finding of the Child Jesus in the Temple

His mother kept all these things in her heart.
Luke 2:51

Sin is the loss of Jesus, and since Mary felt the sting of His absence she could understand the gnawing heart of every sinner and be to it, in the truest sense of the words, "refuge of sinner."
Archbishop Fulton J. Sheen,
The World's First Love

In Mary's Steps

My soul seeks you, my Lord,
as ardently
and urgently
as Mary once sought you
within Jerusalem's staunch walls.

I will rise now and go about the city,
in the streets and in the squares;
I will seek him whom my soul loves.

II
How lost that virgin mother was
without your familiar presence at her side!

I too grieve when I feel your absence,
yearning and longing for your closeness,
my heart afire with desire (and need) for you.

O daughters of Jerusalem,
if you find my beloved,
tell him I am sick with love.

III
Hide not yourself from me, O Lord!
Take not your love from me
nor your Spirit,
for without these mercies
(unmerited gifts you've so graciously given me)
I am desolate and lost.

O satisfy my seeking, Lord,
and reveal yourself to me
(with even but a faint shadow of your splendor and your glory)
that my blind eyes might see again
and my sight be strengthened
for that bright vision of you throughout eternity.

When I found him whom my soul loves,
I held him, and would not let him go.

Luke 2:41-52 The Scene

2:41 Now his parents went to Jerusalem every year at the feast of the Passover. 42 And when he was twelve years old, they went up according to custom; 43 and when the feast was ended, as they were returning, the boy Jesus stayed behind in Jerusalem. His parents did not know it, 44 but supposing him to be in the company they went a day's journey, and they sought him among their kinsfolk and acquaintances; 45 and when they did not find him, they returned to Jerusalem, seeking him.

46 After three days they found him in the temple, sitting among the teachers, listening to them and asking them questions; 47 and all who heard him were amazed at his understanding and his answers. 48 And when they saw him they were astonished; and his mother said to him, "Son, why have you treated us so? Behold, your father and I have been looking for you anxiously." 49 And he said to them, "How is it that you sought me? Did you not know that I must be in my Father's house?" 50 And they did not understand the saying which he spoke to them.

51 And he went down with them and came to Nazareth, and was obedient to them; and his mother kept all these things in her heart. 52 And Jesus increased in wisdom and in stature, and in favor with God and man.

Reflecting on the Word

In the only incident from Jesus' childhood recounted in the Gospels, we once again see the holy family on the road together in obedience to God's command. Their pilgrimage to Jerusalem to celebrate the Passover is a happier trip than the flight into Egypt, yet it too becomes clouded with pain.

All adult Jewish males were to observe the great festivals of Passover, Pentecost, and Tabernacles each year in Jerusalem (Exodus 23:14-17; Deuteronomy 16:16). However, those who lived more than a day's journey from the Holy City were only obliged to make a pilgrimage there once a year. Faithful to the law, Joseph regularly took his family on the eighty-mile trip from Nazareth to Jerusalem for the Passover festivities (Luke 2:41)—a distance that required four to five days to cover. This year, Jesus was especially eager to listen to the teachers in the temple because he was preparing, with Joseph's help, to take up his responsibility to keep the law at age thirteen, becoming a "son of the commandments." (The contemporary Jewish practice of *bar mitzvah* was not yet observed in Jesus' time, but it is rooted in this legal obligation.)

A first-century Jewish family was like a clan, not simply a nuclear household of one set of parents and their children, so many of Mary and Joseph's relatives and friends accompanied them in the caravan from Nazareth to Jerusalem. Just imagine: Jesus probably knew a host of aunts and uncles and cousins, maybe even his grandparents and great-grandparents! But when the feast was over and the weary pilgrims headed back home, their journey was suddenly disrupted: The boy Jesus was nowhere to be found in the company (Luke 2:43-44).

Caravans traveled in two groups, men and women, and the children moved freely between them, so neither Mary nor Joseph noticed their son's absence until camp was set up at the end of the day. Any mother who has lost her child for even a few minutes in a crowded shopping mall can understand Mary's concern when she realizes that Jesus is missing. Had he wandered off along the road, curious as any healthy twelve-year-old, and then lost his way or been injured in a fall? Had he stayed behind in the crowded city, packed well beyond its usual population with the influx of feast-day pilgrims—and maybe some pickpockets and kidnappers as well? Did Mary and Joseph wonder why Jesus left them? Were they in anguish that they had been careless of the trust God had placed in them to care for *his* Son? What a sleepless night they must have had before retracing their steps the next morning to look for him! Or perhaps the anxious couple immediately set out, searching in the darkness.

Students and disciples commonly engaged with the rabbis and masters in question-and-answer sessions and discussions in the temple precincts. Jesus was not precociously presiding over the scene—he was there as an avid listener (Luke 2:46). What sort of queries did this child and the elders of Israel put to each other? Luke notes that all who heard him were amazed at his understanding (2:47). Much later in Jesus' public life, many will again marvel at his wisdom as he teaches with authority (Matthew 7:28; Mark 1:22). In this childhood episode, we can see a foreshadowing of future conversations between Jesus and the leaders of the Jewish nation.

After searching anxiously, the worried parents find their child safe in the temple (Luke 2:48). As St. Bernard of Clairvaux depicted the encounter:

> [Our Lady] calls God Almighty, the Lord of angels, her Son when she asks in all simplicity: "Son, why have you treated us so?" What angel would dare to say such a thing? . . . But Mary, fully aware of her motherhood, does not hesitate to call the Lord of heaven and earth "her Son." And God is not offended for being called what He wanted to be. (*Homilies on the Blessed Virgin Mary*, I, 7)

Jesus, for his part, had not been lost or unsure of his way. Rather, he confidently and clearly points out to his mother that his life's mission is to do his Father's will. "How is it that you sought me? Did you not know that I must be in my Father's house?" (Luke 2:49).

These are the first words of Jesus recorded in the Gospels. The original Greek can also be translated, "I must be about my Father's business." Though Mary does not grasp what Jesus means by his answer (2:50), she offers no further objection to the anxiety he had caused them. Her response is not a closed, offended silence, but an attentive stillness as she turns over in her mind the mystery of her son's identity and his strange words (2:51).

Jesus returns to Nazareth, obedient to the parents God has given him (Luke 2:51). As St. Augustine wrote: "Christ, to whom the universe is subject, was subject to them" (*Sermon 51*, 19). Yet the whole of Jesus' life is a greater act of obedience to the Father: "My food is to do the will of him who sent me, and to accomplish his work" (John 4:34; see also John 5:30). And during the years of Jesus' hidden life at Nazareth, Mary "lived in an intimacy with the mystery of her Son, and went forward in her 'pilgrimage of faith,' while Jesus 'increased in wisdom . . . and in favor with God and man'" (Pope John Paul II, *Redemptoris Mater*, 17).

The next time Luke portrays Jesus on his way to Jerusalem (Luke 9:51), it will once more be to observe the feast there. On that final trip to the Holy City, Jesus will again be found teaching in the temple and responding to the questions posed to him by the Jewish leaders (Luke 20–21)—and there his own Passover will be fulfilled, with his mother once more at his side.

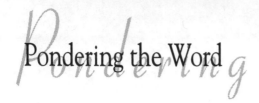

Pondering the Word

1. The holy family observed the Passover in Jerusalem in accordance with the Mosaic law. How do you think their observance of Jewish rituals formed their hearts and minds?

_____

_____

_____

_____

_____

_____

_____

_____

_____

2. The scene in the temple highlights the young Jesus' concern to carry out the Father's will and fulfill his mission. What do Jesus' actions among the teachers tell you about his understanding of himself? How do you think he came to an awareness of his mission?

_____

_____

_____

_____

_____

_____

_____

_____

_____

3. What do Mary's words to Jesus (Luke 2:48) reveal about her as a mother? About her relationship with her son? What insight does Jesus' response to Mary give you into his relationship with God? With his mother?

_____

_____

_____

_____

_____

_____

_____

_____

_____

_____

4. Mary "kept all these things in her heart" (Luke 2:51). What do you think these "things" were? Why was this incident so memorable for Mary and Joseph?

_____

_____

_____

_____

_____

_____

_____

_____

_____

_____

5. Imagine Jesus' life as he grew up in Nazareth as vividly as you can. In what ways do you think he expressed his obedience to his parents (Luke 2:51)?

_____

_____

_____

_____

_____

_____

_____

_____

_____

Living the Word

1. Have you ever been lost? If so, how did it happen and how did you feel? What did you learn from this experience?

lost - found life again through the Bible.

2. Have you ever felt that you have "lost" God through sin or through your own lukewarmness? What did you do to "find" him again?

Bible

3. Jesus recognized God's call on his life to be about his Father's work. Is there a particular call or mission for your life that you feel God has given you? How can you better carry out that mission? Write a prayer dedicating yourself to God and asking for his guidance in your life.

Children- born + unborn

4. How willing are you to reflect over puzzling situations and ponder them patiently, as Mary did? How can you better accept God's ways in your life and in the lives of your loved ones, even when you don't understand them?

Be more patient + ponder

5. Luke describes the child Jesus as growing in wisdom and "in favor with God and man" (Luke 2:52). In what areas of your life would you like to grow more? Ask the Holy Spirit to help you. In what ways do you experience God's pleasure in you?

Jesus- family values teachings

~Brett

6. If you are a parent, what have you learned from this story about how to relate to your children?

Mary: A Portrait of Ardent Longing and Desire for God

How distressed Mary must have been when she realized Jesus was not in the caravan! She was so accustomed to her child's presence, and now he was gone. As a mother, she was concerned for Jesus' safety—after all, the boy was only twelve and some danger might easily have befallen him in the city. But perhaps Mary also felt estranged from her son, wondering in her heart why he had left them. His absence was so sudden and unexpected. Seeking Jesus ardently was the only response Mary could take to satisfy the profound emptiness she must have experienced.

Occasionally we "lose" our awareness of God's presence in us. Perhaps it's because of our busyness, our indifference, or a pattern of sin in our lives. Or perhaps God is "absenting" himself to increase our hunger for him. "If our Lord withdraws himself from the sight of a soul that loves him," explained St. Alphonsus Liguori, "he does not, therefore, depart from the heart; he often conceals himself from a soul, that it may seek him with a more ardent desire and greater love" (*The Glories of Mary*).

Mary sought her missing son with longing and perseverance, not giving up her search until she found him. "Learn, then, from Mary, to seek Jesus," advised Origen, a third-century Christian writer (*Homilies on Luke*,

18). Following in Mary's steps, we too seek Jesus, desiring to embrace him as she did.

Read and prayerfully reflect these additional passages that express longing for the Lord and the satisfaction of "finding" him:

Hear, O LORD, when I cry aloud,
    be gracious to me and answer me!
Thou hast said, "Seek ye my face."
    My heart says to thee,
"Thy face, LORD, do I seek."
    Hide not thy face from me.
(Psalm 27:7-9)

O God, thou art my God, I seek thee,
    my soul thirsts for thee;
my flesh faints for thee,
    as in a dry and weary land where
        no water is.
So I have looked upon thee in the
        sanctuary,
    beholding thy power and glory.
Because thy steadfast love is
        better than life,
    my lips will praise thee.
So I will bless thee as long as I live;
    I will lift up my hands and call on
        thy name. (Psalm 63:1-4)

My soul yearns for thee in the night, my spirit within me earnestly seeks thee. (Isaiah 26:9)

You will seek me and find me; when you seek me with all your heart, I will be found by you, says the LORD. (Jeremiah 29:13-14)

Now after the sabbath, toward dawn of the first day of the week, Mary Magda-lene and the other Mary went to see the sepulchre. . . . The angel said to the women, "Do not be afraid; for I know that you seek Jesus who was crucified. He is not here; for he has risen, as he said. Come, see the place where he lay. Then go quickly and tell his disciples that he has risen from the dead, and behold, he is going before you to Galilee; there you will see him." (Matthew 28:1,5-7)

The Bride:
Another Portrait of Ardent Longing and Desire for God

Read Song of Solomon 3:1-4; 5:6

The Song of Solomon celebrates the love and longing of a man and woman for each other. Yet it is also an allegory of the relationship between God and his people, and between Christ and his church. Moreover, throughout the ages, many saints and mystics—among them Bernard of Clairvaux, Thomas Aquinas, and Teresa of Avila—saw in it a depiction of the soul's quest for union with Christ, the Bridegroom.

The bride of the Song ardently seeks out the beloved: "I will rise now and go about the city, in the streets and in the squares; I will seek him whom my soul loves" (Song of Solomon 3:2). As Jesuit commentator Blaise Arminjon points out, "It is understandable that very often this passage of the Song was applied by the Fathers of the Church to the anxious search for Jesus by his mother throughout the streets of Jerusalem" (*The Cantata of Love*). No effort was too great for the bride to make in searching for her absent bridegroom. Like Mary, she would not rest until she found him whom she loved so dearly. What joy and relief the bride knew when her beloved was once again near her, his presence at her side a source of comfort and strength (3:3-4)!

A Reading from *The Reed of God* by Caryll Houselander

Our Lady's Seeking

Mary and Joseph took the road back to Jerusalem seeking Christ. They looked for Him, as Mary told Him, sorrowing. "Thy Father and I have sought thee sorrowing."

If you have ever loved anyone deeply and then lost him through separation, estrangement, or even by death, you will know that there is an instinct to look for him in every crowd.

The human heart is not reasonable; it will go on seeking for those whom it loves even when they are dead. It will miss a beat when someone passes by who bears them the least resemblance: a tilt of the hat, an uneven walk, a note in the voice.

When St. Augustine was a boy he lost his dearest friend, and he had to leave the town where they had lived together because it became an obsession with him, this looking for the faintest likeness to the dead friend in the crowds thronging the streets that he had once walked in.

Mary and Joseph must have looked into every face of those crowds streaming out of Jerusalem, with even more hunger and sorrow than the heartbroken Augustine. . . .

There would have been no doubt whatever of Our Lady's knowing her son's face; but often, in the dusk, she must have searched for it in the face of another boy, and the boy would have wondered who this woman was and why she leaned down and searched his face; he could not have guessed that the day would come when the Mother of God would really find her son in every boy and every boy would be able to give Christ back to her.

Her search did not end when she found Him in the temple, and it did not really begin when she lost Him on the road from Jerusalem.

From the hour when Gabriel saluted her, the little girl in Nazareth, she had had to seek for Him through faith: to believe that he was in her; to believe that this little child whom she rocked to sleep was God; that it was God whom she taught to walk, to speak, to hold a spoon.

After the finding in the temple He returned to Nazareth and was obedient to her and Joseph. She had to believe that it was God who obeyed them; God who grew and who increased in wisdom.

Later on, she was again seeking for Christ, this time among the crowd that thronged round Him in His public life. She is among those who are trying to get close to Him: therefore, she is among the sick, the crippled, the blind, the poorest beggars—outcasts of every description. For such are the people who follow Christ in every age.

It is just like Our Lady, this: she, who did not seek an exalted or solitary life in which to prepare for Christ's birth, is content now to follow Him in the crowd, to seek Him among strangers in the public street.

The few glimpses that we have of Our Lady nearly all show her in the crowd: crowded out of the inns in Bethlehem, when Christ was born; seeking Him in the crowds on the road back to Jerusalem; persuading Him to His first miracle at a crowded marriage feast; seeking Him in the crowd in His public life. Even in the immense loneliness on Calvary she was surrounded by the crowd around the Cross.

She had followed the crowd to Calvary, but while most of the people stood a little way off, to mock, to stare, to become hysterical with blood lust and the hatred of goodness—some perhaps to mourn for Him, but at a little distance—she passed through them at last, and at last came close to Him.

She stood at the foot of the Cross: not to mourn—that would have been far too small, far too remote from Him, for the sharing in the Passion which was her part—she came there to die—to stand quietly by the Cross and die.

The first great finding was in the temple.

The second great finding was on Calvary.

"Did you not know that I must be about my Father's business?"

"Father, I have finished the work that you gave me to do."

Mary found her lost Child on Calvary.

The Wedding at Cana

Do whatever he tells you.
John 2:5

At Cana, Mary appears once more as the Virgin in prayer: when she tactfully told her Son of a temporal need, she also obtained an effect of grace, namely, that Jesus, in working the first of his "signs," confirmed his disciples' faith in him.
Pope Paul VI,
Marialis Cultus, 18

Mary's Bidding

"They have no wine."

Want and insufficiency
intruded like unwelcome company
at the feast in Cana,
threatening to steal from the newlyweds
the joy that had filled them
as they stood beneath the wedding canopy.
Their hospitality ran too quickly dry,
and the young bride's gentle blush of pleasure
at her guests' merriment
was deepening to a scarlet flush of shame
when suddenly the wine began to flow again.
How many toasts were then drunk in wonderment
and how many lives forever changed
(like that water made, at a word, the best of wine)?

For Mary saw the need that day
and bid her son a favor,
first of those countless she will ask
till all are seated at the marriage supper of the Lamb.

II
I too am visited with frequency
by lack and insufficiency.

My own reserves so quickly fail,
whether that charity
crushed like grapes in the winepress of my soul
and poured out
to refresh the worn and weary
and revive sad hearts,
or that vintage
drunk so eagerly

to quench my parched desires
(or spilled heedlessly upon the ground
as if in libation to my pleasure-gods).
Yet my emptiness is replenished
and all thirst satisfied,
when water is for me
again turned into the best of wine.

For Mary saw my need today
and bid her son a favor,
another of the countless she is asking still
till I am seated at the marriage supper of the Lamb.

John 2:1-12 *The Scene*

2:1 On the third day there was a marriage at Cana in Galilee, and the mother of Jesus was there; [2] Jesus also was invited to the marriage, with his disciples. [3] When the wine failed, the mother of Jesus said to him, "They have no wine." [4] And Jesus said to her, "O woman, what have you to do with me? My hour has not yet come." [5] His mother said to the servants, "Do whatever he tells you." [6] Now six stone jars were standing there, for the Jewish rites of purification, each holding twenty or thirty gallons. [7] Jesus said to them, "Fill the jars with water." And they filled them up to the brim. [8] He said to them, "Now draw some out, and take it to the steward of the feast." So they took it.

[9] When the steward of the feast tasted the water now become wine, and did not know where it came from (though the servants who had drawn the water knew), the steward of the feast called the bridegroom [10] and said to him, "Every man serves the good wine first; and when men have drunk freely, then the poor wine; but you have kept the good wine until now." [11] This, the first of his signs, Jesus did at Cana in Galilee, and manifested his glory; and his disciples believed in him.

[12] After this he went down to Capernaum, with his mother and his brothers and his disciples; and there they stayed for a few days.

Reflecting on the Word

"It is a beautiful and consoling thought," wrote Archbishop Fulton Sheen, "that Our Blessed Lord, who came to teach, sacrifice, and urge us to take up our cross daily, should have begun his public life by assisting at a marriage feast" (*The World's First Love*). Throughout the Gospels, we see Jesus' warmth and humanity in his friendships and his enjoyment of a good party. Moreover, in Jesus' attendance at the wedding at Cana, the church sees "the confirmation of the goodness of marriage and the proclamation that thenceforth marriage will be an efficacious sign of Christ's presence" (*Catechism of the Catholic Church*, 1613).

Perhaps it was a close relative of Mary and her son who had invited them to this wedding celebration, since it took place in Cana, a village not far from Nazareth (John 2:1-2). In the Middle East, where hospitality is so highly valued, it would be quite disconcerting for the hosts to run out of wine to serve their guests. But Mary notices the problem even before the wine steward does, and hopes to remedy the awkward situation before the newlyweds are embarrassed. Today, Mary still recognizes our needs before we ourselves do—and is eager to intercede with her son on our behalf.

This is the only occasion in Scripture when Mary asks Jesus to fill a need. She simply says, "They have no wine." Yet, implicit in her request that he do a kind favor for the couple is Mary's expectation that he would do something out of the ordinary—something supernatural. She does not merely expect him, for instance, to send his disciples out to buy more wine. Pope John Paul II points out the depth and significance of Mary's faith:

At Cana, the Blessed Virgin once again showed her total availability to God. At the Annunciation she had contributed to the miracle of the virginal conception by believing in Jesus before seeing him; here, her trust in Jesus' as yet unrevealed power caused him to perform his "first sign," the miraculous transformation of water into wine. (General audience of February 26, 1997)

By her request, Mary is once again giving over her son to God's call on his life, not hindering or holding on to him in any way. In essence, she is releasing Jesus from his home life and bidding him to enter into his public mission. Since the time she and Joseph had found him as a boy doing his Father's work in the temple (Luke 2:49), she knew this day would come. Certainly Mary realizes that Jesus' answer to her appeal will take him far from her: Now he will belong to all those who see this manifestation of his glory and come to believe in him (John 2:11). Eventually he will belong to those who will seek to destroy him (Matthew 27:1). And Mary herself will no longer be simply the mother of Nazareth's carpenter, Jesus, but the mother of all whom her son will redeem by his saving work.

Although Jesus initially replies that his hour "has not yet come" (John 2:4), it is at his mother's prompting that he ultimately acts and begins to reveal himself. Thus Jesus' "hour"—a word which in John's Gospel refers to his redemptive mission, his passion and death, his resurrection and ascension in glory (7:30; 8:20; 12:27; 16:32; 17:1)—draws nearer to its fulfillment.

Mary repeatedly responded with obedience to God's claim on her own life and that of son. How appropriate it is that her last words to be recorded in the Gospels urge others, too, to obey him (John 2:5). John Paul II encourages us to follow them:

> Mary's request: "Do whatever he tells you," keeps its ever timely value for Christians of every age and is destined to renew its marvelous effect in everyone's life. It is an exhortation to trust without hesitation, especially when one does not understand the meaning or benefit of what Christ asks. (General audience of February 26, 1997)

The waiters' prompt obedience to Jesus' directions to undertake a mundane, practical task opened the way for his creative power to effect a miraculous transformation of 120 gallons of ordinary water into fine wine (John 2:7-10).

In the prophecies of the Old Testament, an abundance of wine is a symbol of the messianic era to come (Isaiah 25:6; Amos 9:13-14; Joel 3:18). In the New Testament, this messianic age is likened to a wedding banquet (Matthew 22:1-14; Revelation 19:9). Thus, Jesus' miracle of producing wine in plenty at a marriage feast points to his identity as the Messiah and to what he is to accomplish by his life and death. Changing the water held in jars used for Jewish ritual purification and the ceremonial washings further implies that the messianic times have now begun. With this "new wine," Jesus inaugurates a new era in God's relationship with his people (Matthew 9:15; Mark 2:22; Luke 5:38). All those who witness this "sign" are invited to faith in the one whom God sent to fulfill his plan of salvation (John 2:11).

"After this," John tells us, "[Jesus] went down to Capernaum, with his mother and his brothers and his disciples; and there they stayed for a few days" (John 2:12). Imagine how Mary must have enjoyed this time with her son and his new companions! We wonder what they all excitedly said to one another in the afterglow of his first miracle. Yet, for this mother, a shadow already hangs over these days as Jesus stands on the threshold of his ministry, for she knows a hard way surely lies ahead of him.

Pondering the Word

1. Why do you think Mary was concerned that the wine was running out? What do you think inspired her to turn to Jesus for a solution to the problem?

felt bad for couple - wanted to help
Maybe she knew it should be the
beginning of His public life.

2. In Jesus' culture, "woman" was a title of respect used in a solemn or formal way. Jesus addressed Mary as "woman" at Cana, at the beginning of his public life (John 2:4), and also at Golgotha, at the end of his life (John 19:26). Why do you think he used this form of address? Read Genesis 3:15 as you consider your answer.

God called her woman

3. What impact did this miracle have on the relationship between Jesus and his mother? Between Jesus and his disciples?

_____

_____

_____

_____

_____

_____

_____

_____

_____

4. Reflect on the various dimensions of Mary's role as mother and intercessor. What do the following titles that she has been given by the church mean to you: "Mother of All People" and "Advocate"?

_____

_____

_____

_____

_____

_____

_____

_____

5. What do the results following the servants' actions suggest about the importance of faith? Of obedience? What other miraculous events in the Gospels required specific actions to be taken before they occurred?

_____

_____

_____

_____

_____

_____

_____

_____

_____

6. John calls the Cana miracle "the first of [Jesus'] signs" (John 2:11). Read about some of Jesus' other miracles in John's Gospel (4:46-54; 5:2-9; 6:4-13; 6:16-21; 9:1-41; and 11:1-44). What made them "signs" of the coming kingdom of God?

_____

_____

_____

_____

_____

_____

_____

_____

Living the Word

1. Mary pointed out the shortage of wine to Jesus, but then left it to him to respond to this need in his own way. Think of at least one situation in your life when you needed to trust in Jesus as Mary did.

_____

_____

_____

_____

_____

_____

_____

_____

2. How ready are you to "do whatever he tells you" (John 2:5)? Is there one particular thing that God is asking you to do? What could help you to respond willingly, especially if you don't understand fully why God is asking this?

_____

_____

_____

_____

_____

_____

_____

3. This miracle underscores Jesus' concern for the practical things that affect our well-being or give us pleasure. In what ways have you experienced God's attention to small details in your life and his abundant provision for you? Has God ever done something for you that seemed to have no other purpose than simply to delight you?

_____

_____

_____

_____

_____

_____

_____

_____

_____

_____

4. The disciples "believed in him" after they saw Jesus transform water into wine at Cana (John 2:11). Recall instances in your life, or in the lives of those around you, when your faith deepened because you recognized God's actions.

_____

_____

_____

_____

_____

_____

_____

_____

_____

5. In this episode, we see how Mary "let go" of her son as he entered his public ministry. In what ways has God asked you to let go of various people who have a significant role in your life? What has helped you to be able to do this freely?

6. Reflect on Mary's role in your own life. In what ways have you experienced her intercession for you? Write a prayer or a letter to Mary expressing your love and gratitude to her.

Rooted in the Word

Mary: A Portrait of an Intercessor

In his *Sunday Sermons*, St. Alphonsus Liguori eloquently reflects on Mary's charity and compassion that moved her to be concerned for those whom she saw in need:

> To understand Mary's great goodness, let us remember what the Gospel says. . . . There was a shortage of wine, which naturally worried the married couple. No one asks the Blessed Virgin to intervene and request her Son to come to the rescue of the couple. But Mary's heart cannot but take pity on the unfortunate couple; . . . it stirs her to act as intercessor and ask her Son for the miracle, even though no one asks her to. . . . If our Lady acted like this without being asked, what would she not have done if they actually asked her to intervene? (48)

Mary's intercession has continued beyond her earthly life. Now in heaven, she intercedes for us with maternal love. There, as our advocate, she pleads our cause and presents our petitions before the throne of God. She also asks God to look with mercy and forgiveness on our sins and to protect us against temptations and dangers.

The earliest known prayer to Mary, the *Sub tuum praesidium* from the third or fourth century, implored her help: "We fly to thy patronage, O holy Mother of God. Despise not our petitions in our necessities, but deliver us from all danger, O ever glorious and blessed Virgin." More familiar to us today are the Rosary and the *Memorare*, prayers in which we honor Mary as well as call upon her to intercede for us. In imitation of Mary, we too are to lift up one another before God in prayer and intercession.

Read and prayerfully reflect on these additional passages that describe the power and effects of intercession:

[Moses] prayed to the LORD, "O Lord GOD, destroy not thy people and thy heritage, whom thou hast redeemed through thy greatness, whom thou hast brought out of Egypt with a mighty hand. Remember thy servants, Abraham, Isaac, and Jacob; do not regard the stubbornness of this people, or their wickedness, or their sin." (Deuteronomy 9:26-27)

If God is for us, who is against us? He who did not spare his own Son but gave him up for us all, will he not also give us all things with him? Who shall bring any charge against God's elect? It is God who justifies; who is to condemn? Is it Christ

Jesus, who died, yes, who was raised from the dead, who is at the right hand of God, who indeed intercedes for us? (Romans 8:31-34)

Christ has entered, not into a sanctuary made with hands, a copy of the true one, but into heaven itself, now to appear in the presence of God on our behalf. (Hebrews 9:24)

Without ceasing I mention you always in my prayers (Romans 1:9)

I urge that supplications, prayers, intercessions, and thanksgivings be made for all men . . . This is good, and it is acceptable in the sight of God our Savior, who desires all men to be saved and to come to the knowledge of the truth. (1 Timothy 2:1, 3-4)

Esther: Another Portrait of an Intercessor

Read Esther 3:7–5:8; 7:1–8:8

Queen Esther has been recognized traditionally by the church as a type or prefigurement of Mary. Through her faith and courageous trust in God, an evil plot against the Jewish people was defeated and their destruction averted. This points to how Mary, centuries later, played a key part in God's plan of salvation by believing in his word. Through her son, Satan was defeated and the human race was redeemed from sin and eternal death.

Esther also prefigures Mary in her role as intercessor. This Jewish queen once came before the throne of a king to ask for salvation and mercy, just as Mary does now before God's throne in heaven. Esther, however, had to take her life into her hands to intercede on behalf of her people, because it was against the law—the penalty was death—to come into King Ahasuerus' presence without being summoned. After asking the Jews to fast on her behalf, Esther dared to present herself at the royal court.

Queen Esther found favor in the king's sight and won her suit. Ultimately, King Ahasuerus granted her petition to save the Jews—but Esther risked her life to gain a hearing. How blessed we are that now, through the blood of Jesus, we can come freely into the presence of our divine King and God, confident that he loves us and that he will hear our petitions!

A Reading from *The World's First Love* by Archbishop Fulton J. Sheen

The Marriage Feast of Cana

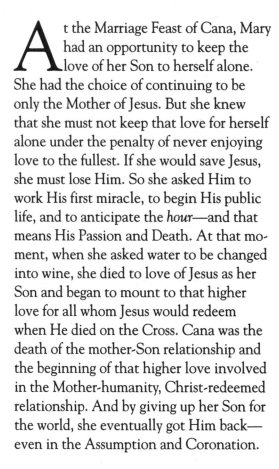

At the Marriage Feast of Cana, Mary had an opportunity to keep the love of her Son to herself alone. She had the choice of continuing to be only the Mother of Jesus. But she knew that she must not keep that love for herself alone under the penalty of never enjoying love to the fullest. If she would save Jesus, she must lose Him. So she asked Him to work His first miracle, to begin His public life, and to anticipate the *hour*—and that means His Passion and Death. At that moment, when she asked water to be changed into wine, she died to love of Jesus as her Son and began to mount to that higher love for all whom Jesus would redeem when He died on the Cross. Cana was the death of the mother-Son relationship and the beginning of that higher love involved in the Mother-humanity, Christ-redeemed relationship. And by giving up her Son for the world, she eventually got Him back—even in the Assumption and Coronation.

The end of all human love is doing the will of God. Even the most frivolous speak of love in terms of eternity. Love is timeless. As true love develops, there are at first two loves facing one another, seeking to possess one another. As love progresses, the two loves, instead of seeking one another, seek an object outside both. They both develop a passion for unity outside of themselves, namely, in God. That is why, as a pure Christian love matures, a husband and spouse become more and more religious as time goes on. At first the happiness consisted in doing the will of the other; then the happiness consisted in doing the will of God. True love is a religious act. If I love you as God wills that I love you, it is the highest expression of love.

The last words of Mary that were spoken in Sacred Scripture were the words of total abandonment to the will of God. "Whatsoever He shall say to you, that do ye." As Dante said: "In His will is our peace." Love has no other destiny than to obey Christ. Our wills are ours only to give away. The human heart is torn between a sense of emptiness and a need of being filled, like the water pots of Cana. The emptiness comes from the fact that we are human. The power of filling belongs only to Him Who ordered the water pots filled. Lest any heart should fail in being filled, Mary's last valedictory is: "Whatsoever He shall say to you, that do ye." The heart has the need of emptying and a need of being filled. The power of emptying is human— emptying in the love of others; the power of filling belongs only to God. Hence all perfect love must end on the note: "Not my will, but Thine be done, O Lord!"

At the Foot of the Cross

Behold, your mother!
John 19:27

Only a consistency that lasts throughout the whole of life can be called faithfulness. Mary's *fiat* in the Annunciation finds its fullness in the silent *fiat* that she repeats at the foot of the cross.
Pope John Paul II, Homily delivered in Mexico, January 26, 1979

Pietà

How sore your grief, Mary,
as you hold the cold and lifeless body of your son
(once warm with beating heart in your own womb)
all bloodied now by death,
and cradle in your arms for one last time
him whom you so often held upon your breast.

Sharing in his pain and passion,
you looked on in agony
as the hands that clung as infant's around your neck
and those feet that pattered long ago about the cozy home in Nazareth
were cruelly wrenched and nailed fast.

I wonder:

Had you spoken in quiet hours together
of the prophecies and their mysteries?
Had you—with motherly intuition—
read your son's heart and the shadow that hung over him?
In your nights of pondering,
did you gather strength for this inevitable day?

And now, with a mother's knowing heart,
can you perceive that this stiffening form upon your lap
(a piece of torn humanity that tabernacles divinity within)
will soon breathe again
and brim and pulse with life,
all gloriously transfigured?

Looking through the darkness there at Golgotha,
do you already see in your mind's eye
the new dawn promised in three days' time
and tremble to feel again your child's glad embrace?

O wait no longer, Mary,
to entrust him to the grave!
Surrender your son now to Joseph's tomb,
that he might rest awhile from the battle bravely fought
and then descend to death's domain
to claim from Satan there
the victory so hard won for us.

John 19:25-30 The Scene

ask Susie →

19:25 Standing by the cross of Jesus were his mother, and his mother's sister, Mary the wife of Clopas, and Mary Magdalene. 26 When Jesus saw his mother, and the disciple whom he loved standing near, he said to his mother, "Woman, behold, your son!" 27 Then he said to the disciple, "Behold, your mother!" And from that hour the disciple took her to his own home.

28 After this Jesus, knowing that all was now finished, said (to fulfill the scripture), "I thirst." 29 A bowl full of vinegar stood there; so they put a sponge full of the vinegar on hyssop and held it to his mouth. 30 When Jesus had received the vinegar, he said, "It is finished"; and he bowed his head and gave up his spirit.

Luke 23:44-56 The Scene

23-44 It was now about the sixth hour, and there was darkness over the whole land until the ninth hour, 45 while the sun's light failed; and the curtain of the temple was torn in two. 46 Then Jesus, crying with a loud voice, said, "Father, into thy hands I commit my spirit!" And having said this he breathed his last.

47 Now when the centurion saw what had taken place, he praised God, and said, "Certainly this man was innocent!" 48 And all the multitudes who assembled to see the sight, when they saw what had taken place, returned home beating their breasts. 49 And all his acquaintances and the women who had followed him from Galilee stood at a distance and saw these things.

50 Now there was a man named Joseph from the Jewish town of Arimathea. He was a member of the council, a good and righteous man, 51 who had not consented to their purpose and deed, and he was looking for the kingdom of God. 52 This man went to Pilate and asked for the body of Jesus. 53 Then he took it down and wrapped it in a linen shroud, and laid him in a rock-hewn tomb, where no one had ever yet been laid. 54 It was the day of Preparation, and the sabbath was beginning. 55 The women who had come with him from Galilee followed, and saw the tomb, and how his body was laid; 56 then they returned, and prepared spices and ointments. On the sabbath they rested according to the commandment.

Reflecting on the Word

Mary's request at Cana had set her son on his public course. In the months that followed, she must have heard about the miracles Jesus was working throughout the region. And at least once, she and his relatives sought him out. Jesus had said then, "My mother and my brethren are those who hear the word of God and do it" (Luke 8:21), thus recognizing Mary not only as his mother according to the flesh but as a true disciple.

Might Jesus also have stopped by to see his mother when he preached in the synagogue at Nazareth? His hometown had little regard for his new activities (Matthew 13:53-58), but Mary would not have been surprised that some spoke against her son. Hadn't Simeon long ago predicted that many would oppose him (Luke 2:34)? Recalling the old priest's words, she knew, too, that more sorrows were still to pierce her heart (2:35).

Perhaps Mary accompanied Jesus and the band of disciples on his last journey to Jerusalem to celebrate the Passover (Luke 9:51; 13:22). Was she in the crowd crying "Hosanna" as he entered the Holy City (Matthew 21:1-11)? Did she stay with his dear friends Martha, Mary, and Lazarus in Bethany (Luke 10:38-39; John 11:1-3; 12:1-3)? In any case, Mary was near enough to receive the news when Jesus was arrested—and she comes to him now at Golgotha.

There, at the place of execution, Mary's faith is stretched to the utmost. Pain courses through her own body and soul as she watches her son—flesh of her flesh—being tortured so horribly. She can only look on in anguish, unable to wipe the sweat and spittle and blood from Jesus' face as his body sags against the nails. Yet Mary stands resolutely by his cross (John 19:25). Her unconditional yes—first given when she united her will to the Father's and the Word became flesh in her—prepared her to trust God unquestioningly. The years since then of repeatedly embracing God's ways do not now lessen the sharpness of her pain but, steeped in her consent, she accepts the price that must be paid so that God's plan of salvation can be accomplished.

From the cross, Jesus speaks to his mother and his beloved disciple, John. As Pope John Paul II explains, the Lord's words show more than a final act of kindness to provide for Mary's care after he was gone:

The words of the dying Jesus actually show that his first intention was not to entrust his Mother to John, but to entrust the disciple to Mary and to give her a new maternal role. . . . The reality brought about by Jesus' words, that is, Mary's new motherhood in relation to the disciple, is a further sign of the great love that led Jesus to offer his life for all people. On Calvary this love was shown in the gift of a mother, his mother, who thus became our mother too. We must remember that, according to tradition, the Blessed Virgin recognized John as her son. But this privilege has been interpreted by Christians from the beginning as the sign of a spiritual generation in relation to all humanity. (General audience of May 7, 1997)

Writing in the sixteenth century, Augustinian friar Venerable Thomas of Jesus had similarly described Mary's new maternal role and its significance:

The holy virgin . . . entered fully into her Son's intentions, assumed the heart of a mother for all sinners, and looked upon them as the children of sorrow whom she had brought forth at the foot of the cross. Thus that sea of sufferings into which Jesus and Mary were plunged has become for sinners a river of peace and a fountain of blessings. (*The Sufferings of Jesus*)

On a natural level, Jesus entrusts his mother to John so that he will take care of her and she will extend her maternal care to him. But in a deeper way, Jesus creates a new family: The church is born as he dies. Here at Golgotha, at the fulfillment of his "hour" by his glorification on the cross (John 17:1-5), Mary's maternal role takes on a universal dimension in a motherhood that extends to all humanity. Jesus gives up everything as he dies, including his mother. But, as Archbishop Fulton Sheen observed, "He would find her again, mothering His Mystical Body" (*The World's First Love*).

"From that hour the disciple took her to his home" (John 19:27). More than simply pro-viding her with a place to live, John will bring Mary into his life. We, too, are invited to follow the example of the disciple "whom Jesus loved" (13:23) and make a special place for Mary in our own lives.

Also standing near the cross of Jesus were "his mother's sister, Mary the wife of Clopas, and Mary Magdalene" (John 19:25). Mark offers another list of those present: "There were also women looking on from afar, among whom were Mary Magdalene, and Mary the mother of James the younger and of Joses, and Salome, who, when he was in Galilee, followed him, and ministered to him; and also many other women who came up with him to Jerusalem" (Mark 15:40-41). These women stay with Jesus to the end with loving devotion and unshaken loyalty. Theirs is a love that continues to flow from the heart even when the mind is stunned and confused, a love that seeks to comfort Jesus simply by being present. Perhaps we owe a great debt to them, for they may have been the witnesses who supplied the early church with the detailed account of the crucifixion and Jesus' words from that cross that we still read today.

These faithful women had cared for Jesus in his life (Luke 8:3), and now they want to care for him in his burial: They prepare spices, hoping to anoint Jesus' body with them in one final gesture of love after the day of rest (Mark 15:47–16:1; Luke 23:55–24:1). And in the silence of the sabbath, Mary waits in faith and hope, sustained by a love stronger than death.

Pondering the Word

1. Jesus first mentioned his "hour" at Cana (John 2:4) and spoke frequently of it before his crucifixion—for example, see Matthew 26:45-46; John 5:25-29; 12:27-28: 17:1-5. Why do you think Jesus referred to his mission and his crucifixion using a measurement of time? In what way is Jesus' "hour" a point in time and also timeless?

disciples priests?

_____

_____

_____

_____

_____

_____

_____

_____

_____

2. What does Jesus' concern for Mary as he was dying on the cross tell you about his relationship with his mother, both on a natural and supernatural level?

_____

_____

_____

_____

_____

_____

_____

_____

_____

3. How does John 19:25-27 help you understand Mary as "Mother of the Faithful," and "Mother of the Church"? In what way does John represent the church?

Mother of the church

4. Why do you think Jesus chose John as the one to whom he entrusted the care of his mother? Read Mark 14:32-42; Luke 8:49-56; 9:28-36; John 13:23-26; 20:1-10; 21:20-23 to understand more about John and his relationship with Jesus.

5. Do you think that Mary expected Jesus to be executed? That she understood what Jesus was accomplishing through his death on the cross? Why or why not? In what ways do you understand the death of Jesus as necessary for the salvation of humanity? As a triumph?

_____

_____

_____

_____

_____

_____

_____

_____

_____

6. John noted that Mary's sister was with her at the foot of the cross (John 19:25), and he and the other evangelists recorded that Mary Magdalene and several other women who knew Jesus were among those who witnessed his crucifixion (Mark 15:40-41). Based on their presence at Calvary, what conclusions might you draw about these women and their "support network"?

_____

_____

_____

_____

_____

_____

_____

_____

Living the Word

1. Imagine yourself among those who accompanied Jesus on his journeys (Luke 8:2-3) and were present at Golgotha (Mark 15:40-41). What do you think was the impact on their lives from knowing Jesus and following him? How has following Jesus changed your own life?

_____

_____

_____

_____

_____

_____

_____

2. Think of a time in your life when you were experiencing great pain or sorrow. To whom did you turn to find strength and hope? Did your faith in God grow weaker or stronger during that time? Why?

_____

_____

_____

_____

_____

_____

_____

3. In what ways is Mary a "spiritual mother" to you? Have you brought Mary into your home or made a place for her in your life as John did? How has your relationship with her changed and deepened throughout your life?

_____

_____

_____

_____

_____

_____

_____

_____

_____

4. Jesus' own loving care for his mother is a model to us of how to serve others. The women showed their love and care for Jesus by their presence near the cross and by making preparations for his burial. How do you support those who are suffering a serious loss or grieving the death of a loved one? Recall and thank God for those who have "stood near" to you in times of difficulty or sorrow in your own life.

_____

_____

_____

_____

_____

_____

_____

_____

5. After the Good Friday liturgy, the altar is stripped and the empty tabernacle stands open: Christ is no longer present in the church in the Blessed Sacrament. Until the Easter vigil, Christians experience something of the great void that the apostles and the women experienced after Jesus died. Imagine what they might have felt and done on the sabbath after Jesus was laid in the tomb. In what way do you experience this void on Holy Saturday?

Mary: A Portrait of Faithfulness

The mosaic above the Calvary altar in the Church of the Holy Sepulchre shows Mary standing in fortitude, watching as Jesus is nailed to the cross. This is a profoundly moving image—and it is an image that concretely defines what it means to be faithful: firm in faith, loyal, constant, trustworthy, and reliable in performing one's duty.

Mary stood with Jesus to the bitter end. Although she may have been tempted to avoid the trauma of her son's crucifixion, she nevertheless demonstrated her solidarity with her son and his mission by standing at the foot of the cross. The memories of her son's agonies must have stayed with her for the rest of her life, yet she could not abandon him in his hour of need. Throughout her life, Mary's unwavering faithfulness was rooted in her knowledge of God, who is "abounding in steadfast love and faithfulness" (Exodus 34:6). God had been faithful to his promises to her. Strengthened by this knowledge, Mary could stand, as the ancient hymn *Stabat Mater* describes her, "close to Jesus to the last."

Such faithfulness as Mary's is possible only in response to God himself. Yet we too can stand faithfully rooted in God as Mary did, for his steadfast love and faithfulness surround and uphold us.

Read and prayerfully reflect on these additional passages that portray the nature of faithfulness, both divine and human:

Thou, O Lord, art a God merciful and
 gracious,
slow to anger and abounding in
 steadfast love and faithfulness.
(Psalm 86:15)

May the God of peace himself sanctify you wholly; and may your spirit and soul and body be kept sound and blameless at the coming of our Lord Jesus Christ. He who calls you is faithful, and he will do it. (1 Thessalonians 5:23-24)

If we have died with [Christ], we shall also live with him; if we endure, we shall also reign with him; if we deny him, he also will deny us; if we are faithless, he remains faithful—for he cannot deny himself. (2 Timothy 2:11-13)

Let us hold fast the confession of our hope without wavering, for he who promised is faithful. (Hebrews 10:23)

Be faithful unto death, and I will give you the crown of life. (Revelation 2:10)

Priscilla and Aquila: Two Other Portraits of Faithfulness

Read Acts 18

When the emperor Claudius expelled all the Jews from Rome in A.D. 49, Priscilla and her husband, Aquila, settled in Corinth where they met Paul, a tentmaker like themselves (Acts 18:2-3). Inspired by Paul's faith and preaching, they remained faithfully by him when his preaching met with opposition (18:4-17). Priscilla and Aquila accompanied Paul when he set sail on his next journey, weathering the hardships of missionary life with him (18:18). In Ephesus, the couple instructed Apollos in the faith (18:24-26) and became leaders in the local church.

Sometime later Priscilla and Aquila returned to Rome, where they established a house church (Romans 16:3, 5). Paul mentioned them several times in his letters, greeting them warmly and commending them for their faithful service (2 Timothy 4:19; 1 Corinthians 16:19). The apostle was especially grateful to them, because they had even risked their lives to save him (Romans 16:3-4).

The faith of Priscilla and Aquila grew strong and flourished in the midst of difficult circumstances. Among the first Christian missionaries and leaders, they were loyal coworkers of Paul who stood by him and the young Christian church in challenging times. Like Mary, they were firm in their belief in God's word and confident of his saving power. We know them today because of their faithfulness to Christ and his gospel.

A Reading from Romanos the Melodist

Mary at the Cross

A hymn in the form of a dialogue between mother and son at the most dramatic hour of salvation history:

Come, let us all celebrate him who was crucified for us: for Mary looked on him upon the cross and said: "Though you endure crucifixion, yet you are my son, my God."

Worn out with grief, Mary, the ewe, seeing her own lamb taken to the slaughter, followed with the other women and cried: "Where are you going, my child? For whose sake are you finishing this swift race? Is there yet another marriage at Cana, and are you hastening there now to change the water into wine for them? Shall I go with you, child, or shall I rather wait for you? Speak to me, O Word; do not pass me by in silence: for you kept me in my purity, my son, my God. . . . If you heal Adam, and Eve with him, shall I see you again? For my fear is that from the tomb you may hasten to heaven, my child; and I, searching to see you, shall weep and cry out: 'Where is my son, my God?'"

When he who knows of all things before their birth heard this, he answered Mary: "Take courage, mother, for you shall be the first to see me (risen) from the tomb; and I shall come to show you from what suffering I liberated Adam and how much I sweated for his sake. I shall reveal it to my friends and show them the tokens in my hands; and then, mother, you shall see Eve living as before, and you shall cry for joy: 'He saved my parents, my son, my God.'

"Endure a little, mother, and you shall see how I, like a healer, divest myself and come to where they lie, and how I heal their wounds, cutting their calluses and scabs with the lance; and I shall take the vinegar and with it bathe their wounds; I shall open the wound with the chisel (made) of the nails and dress it with the cloak and my cross I shall use, mother, as a splint, that you may sing with understanding: 'By suffering he freed us from suffering, my son, my God.'

"Put aside your grief, mother, put it aside, and go in joy; for now I hasten to fulfill that for which I came, the will of him who sent me. For from the first this was resolved by me and by my Father, and it was never displeasing to my spirit; that I become man and suffer for him who had fallen. Hasten then, mother, and announce to all that 'By suffering he lays low the hater of Adam, and comes as a conqueror, my son, my God.'"

[Mary]: "I am overcome, my child, overcome by love, and truly I cannot bear it, that I am to be in my room while you are on the cross, I within my house, you within the tomb. Therefore let me go with you, for it heals me to look upon you, I shall look upon the outrageous daring of those who honor Moses; for these blind men, pretending to be his avengers, have come here to kill you. But what Moses said to Israel was this: 'You will see life hanging on the cross.' And what is life? My son and my God."

[Jesus]: "If you come with me, mother, do not weep, and do not tremble if you see the elements shaken. For this outrage will make all creation tremble; the sky will be blinded and not open its eyes until I speak; then the earth and the sea together will hasten to disappear, and the temple will rend its veil against the perpetrators of this outrage. The mountains will be shaken, the graves emptied. If, like a woman, you are seized by fear when you see this, cry out with me: 'Spare me, my son, my God.'"

Son of the Virgin, God of the Virgin, and creator of the world: yours is the suffering, yours the depths of wisdom. You know what you were and what you became; because you were willing to suffer, you deigned to come and save mankind. Like a lamb you have lifted our sins from us, and you have abolished them by your sacrifice, my Savior, and saved every man. You exist both in suffering and in not suffering; by dying you save, and you have given to the holy lady freedom to cry to you: "My son and my God."

tecost

All these [apostles] with one accord devoted themselves to prayer, together with the women and Mary the mother of Jesus, and with his brothers.
Acts 1:14

Pentecost . . . reveals the face of the Church as a family gathered together with Mary, enlivened by the outpouring of the Spirit and ready for the mission of evangelization. The contemplation of this scene . . . ought to lead the faithful to an ever greater appreciation of their new life in Christ, lived in the heart of the Church, a life of which the scene of Pentecost itself is the great "icon."
Pope John Paul II,
Rosarium Virginis Mariae, **23**

Pentecost Vigil

Gently came the Spirit
overshadowing Mary
on that bright Annunciation Day
(careful to preserve her young innocence)
and the immensity of God
was conceived within her virgin womb.

Now her child has gone from her,
ascending to his eternal realm
that enfolds all bounds of time and space within itself.
But he gave pledge and surety
to his earthly family not to leave them desolate:
I will pray the Father,
and he will give you another Counselor,
to be with you for ever, even the Spirit of truth.

This virgin mother keeps vigil
(a new *fiat* ready on her lips),
watching for his promise to be fulfilled:
You shall be clothed with power from on high.

In this novena of pregnant nights and days,
do Magdalene and Thomas raise heavenward
hands eager to touch their risen Lord again?
Does Peter still weep contrite tears,
and does Mary
(secure in the care of Christ's beloved John)
wait with an expectant mother's patience
for a new birthing?

160

Then suddenly
a whirlwind invades and fills this upper room
(and all waiting hearts)
with the force and freshness of God's own vitality
and tongues of fire burn upon the charged air.

Her vigil ended,
a new *Magnificat* spills from Mary
as the power of the Most High overshadows her once more
and the church is Spirit-born.

1:12 Then they returned to Jerusalem from the mount called Olivet, which is near Jerusalem, a sabbath day's journey away; 13 and when they had entered, they went up to the upper room, where they were staying, Peter and John and James and Andrew, Philip and Thomas, Bartholomew and Matthew, James the son of Alphaeus and Simon the Zealot and Judas the son of James. 14 All these with one accord devoted themselves to prayer, together with the women and Mary the mother of Jesus, and with his brothers.

2:1 When the day of Pentecost had come, they were all together in one place. 2 And suddenly a sound came from heaven like the rush of a mighty wind, and it filled all the house where they were sitting. 3 And there appeared to them tongues as of fire, distributed and resting on each one of them. 4 And they were all filled with the Holy Spirit and began to speak in other tongues, as the Spirit gave them utterance.

14 But Peter, standing with the eleven, lifted up his voice and addressed them, "Men of Judea and all who dwell in Jerusalem, let this be known to you, and give ear to my words. 15 For these men are not drunk, as you suppose, since it is only the third hour of the day; 16 but this is what was spoken by the prophet Joel:
17 'And in the last days it shall be, God declares,

that I will pour out my Spirit upon all flesh,
and your sons and your daughters shall prophesy,
and your young men shall see visions,
and your old men shall dream dreams;
18 yea, and on my menservants and my maidservants in those days
I will pour out my Spirit; and they shall prophesy.
21 And it shall be that whoever calls on the name of the Lord shall be saved.'"

41 So those who received his word were baptized, and there were added that day about three thousand souls.

42 And they devoted themselves to the apostles' teaching and fellowship, to the breaking of bread and the prayers. 43 And fear came upon every soul; and many wonders and signs were done through the apostles. 44 And all who believed were together and had all things in common; 45 and they sold their possessions and goods and distributed them to all, as any had need. 46 And day by day, attending the temple together and breaking bread in their homes, they partook of food with glad and generous hearts, 47 praising God and having favor with all the people. And the Lord added to their number day by day those who were being saved.

Reflecting on the Word

Where did Mary go after that harrowing day at Golgotha? Did John's family have a home in Jerusalem where he sheltered her as she grieved? We can only wonder where she was and what she thought as she kept the sabbath rest. Addressing "Our Lady of Holy Saturday" in his meditations, Cardinal Carlo Martini of Milan wrote:

> You learnt, O Mary, to wait and to hope. You waited with trust for the birth of the Son that the angel proclaimed; you continued to believe in the word of Gabriel, even during those long periods of time when you understood nothing; you hoped against every hope under the Cross and right up to the Sepulchre itself; during Holy Saturday you instilled hope into the confused and disappointed disciples. Through you, the disciples were given the consolation of hope, the consolation that could be called "the consolation of the heart," and through you our hearts are consoled too. (*Our Lady of Holy Saturday*)

Perhaps the women who went to the tomb to anoint Jesus' body (Luke 24:1-12) ran to Mary with the news that they had seen the risen Lord (Matthew 28:1-10). Although all the evangelists remain silent here, might we suppose—as St. Ignatius of Loyola and Pope John Paul II have suggested—that Jesus came to his mother first of all?

At the Annunciation, Mary opened herself without reserve to the power of the Spirit and to her maternal role. At Pentecost, her motherhood in the Spirit becomes universal: The church not only recognizes Mary as the mother of Jesus but also calls her "Mother of the Church." As Cardinal Joseph Ratzinger points out,

> Mary's motherhood is not just based on the biological event, which happened once, but on the fact that in her total being, Mary was, and is, and therefore will remain, a mother. Pentecost, the birth of the Church by the Holy Spirit, shows this in factual terms: Mary is in the midst of the praying assembly that, by the Spirit's Advent, becomes Church. The analogy between Christ's Incarnation by the power of the Spirit at Nazareth, and the birth of the Church on Pentecost, cannot be disregarded. "The person who links these two moments is Mary" [*Redemptoris Mater*, 24]. (*The Sign of the Woman: An Introduction to the Encyclical*)

First overshadowed by the Holy Spirit (Luke 1:35) at the Annunciation, Mary also experienced the Spirit's presence and work throughout her life. So now, in the upper room, she realizes how much the apostles and other disciples would benefit from the promised coming of the Spirit: It is the Spirit who will equip them to proclaim all that they had witnessed and to preach repentance and the forgiveness of sins in Jesus' name (Luke 24:47-48). Thus, "mindful of Jesus' promise, she waited for Pentecost and implored a multiplicity of gifts for everyone, in accordance with each one's personality and mission" (Pope John Paul II). Further explaining the significance of Mary's prayer for this first Christian community, the pope added:

It fosters the coming of the Spirit, imploring his action in the hearts of the disciples and in the world. Just as in the Incarnation the Spirit had formed the physical body of Christ in her virginal womb, in the upper room the same Spirit came down to give life to the Mystical Body. Thus, Pentecost is also a fruit of the Blessed Virgin's incessant prayer, which is accepted by the Paraclete with special favor because it is an expression of her motherly love for the Lord's disciples. (General audience of May 28, 1997)

Those gathered in the upper room do not wait and pray in vain. True to his word, God sends his Spirit upon these expectant disciples in power manifested by wind and fire—and miraculous speech. In amazement, devout Jews in Jerusalem and visitors from all parts of the world hear the Spirit-filled followers of Jesus "telling in our own language the mighty works of God" (Acts 2:1-11). In this gift of new tongues, the confusion of Babel (Genesis 11:1-9) is reversed as one common word—the word of God—is heard by all.

Filled with this new power, Peter boldly proclaims Jesus of Nazareth—crucified and now raised from the dead—as Lord and Christ (Acts 2:22-36). "Repent," he urges his listeners, "and be baptized every one of you in the name of Jesus Christ for the forgiveness of your sins; and you shall receive the gift of the Holy Spirit" (2:38). About three thousand people received Peter's word and were baptized (2:41)—the newest members of the church that has just been born. A new age begins for the human race as God pours out his Spirit on Pentecost.

Surely we can imagine Mary—her heart filled with joy and gratitude—in the midst of this community of believers (Acts 2:44-47). John Paul II proposes that "after Pentecost her life would have continued to be hidden and discreet, watchful and effective. Since she was enlightened and guided by the Spirit, she exercised a deep influence on the community of the Lord's disciples" (General audience of May 28, 1997).

According to one early Christian tradition, Mary remained in Jerusalem, and the "tomb of the Virgin" is still venerated today in the crypt of the Orthodox Church of the Assumption at the foot of the Mount of

Olives. Another tradition holds that she accompanied John to Ephesus and lived there until the end of her earthly life. Some propose that Mary died a physical death and was resurrected, and then taken bodily into heaven by God; others believe in her "falling asleep" rather than dying, which implies a physical corruption, before she was assumed. The Catholic Church offers no judgment on where, when, or precisely how Mary passed from this life to the next, but clearly states:

> "Finally the Immaculate Virgin, preserved free from all stain of original sin, when the course of her earthly life was finished, was taken up body and soul into heavenly glory, and exalted by the Lord as Queen over all things, so that she might be the more fully conformed to her Son, the Lord of lords and conqueror of sin and death" [*Lumen Gentium*, 59]. The Assumption of the Blessed Virgin is a singular participation in her Son's Resurrection and an anticipation of the resurrection of other Christians. (*Catechism of the Catholic Church*, 966)

Pondering the Word

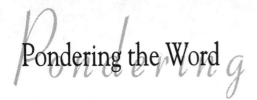

Paraclete-Holy Spirit

1. How did Jesus describe his purposes in sending the Spirit to his disciples? Read John 14:16-29; 16:7-15, Luke 24:45-49, and Acts 1:4-5, 8 as you consider your answer.

_____

_____

_____

_____

_____

_____

_____

_____

2. How do you think Mary's presence in the upper room affected Jesus' disciples as they waited together with her in prayer? What role or influence do you think she had in this group?

_____

_____

_____

_____

_____

_____

_____

_____

_____

3. In your opinion, did Mary and the other followers of Jesus have a clear idea of what to expect with the coming of the Spirit? Why or why not?

_____

_____

_____

_____

_____

_____

_____

_____

4. What elements of the prophecy of Joel (2:28-32) that Peter spoke of in his sermon (Acts 2:14-21) do you see being fulfilled on Pentecost? Is this "fulfillment" visible in the church today?

_____

_____

_____

_____

_____

_____

_____

_____

5. What role did the Spirit play in shaping the early Christian church? Which of the practices and activities described in Acts 2:42-47 do you see present in the life of the church today?

_____

_____

_____

_____

_____

_____

_____

_____

6. In what ways does Mary serve as a model for living a Spirit-filled life? What have you learned from her openness and responsiveness to the Holy Spirit?

_____

_____

_____

_____

_____

_____

_____

_____

Living the Word

1. What has God promised you that you are now waiting for him to give you? How can you place yourself at God's disposal to receive his promise?

_____

_____

_____

_____

_____

_____

_____

_____

_____

2. How does the Holy Spirit manifest his presence through what you do in your relationships with others and in your normal daily activities? Are you ever reluctant to let the Spirit act in your life in new and unexpected ways? If so, why?

_____

_____

_____

_____

_____

_____

_____

_____

3. What quality of Mary or scene from her life made the deepest impression on you during the course of your study and reflection? What title of Mary is most important to you personally? Why? How will you continue to make a place for Mary in your life?

"Queen of Peace"
- Peace with spouse, ...
Peace with family ...
Peace with neighbor ...
Peace with world.

4. Mary has appeared in Lourdes, Fatima, and elsewhere to bring hope to Christians and to guide them to her son. What do these appearances say about Mary's love for humanity and her role as "Mother of the Church"?

5. Write a prayer to Mary, honoring her and asking her, through her example and her intercession, to bring you closer to her son, Jesus.

_____

_____

_____

_____

_____

_____

_____

_____

_____

Every person has been given a guardian angel.

Mary: A Portrait of a Spirit-Filled Disciple

Overshadowed by "the power of the Most High" at the Annunciation and again "clothed with power from on high" on Pentecost (Luke 1:35; 24:49), Mary is the model of a Spirit-filled disciple. Inspired by the Spirit, she was the first to believe in Jesus and to follow him in love and service.

After the Spirit came upon her, those to whom Mary was sent—Elizabeth and her son, John the Baptist—were also touched by the Spirit. Carrying the life of the Messiah in her, she also carried him to others. Throughout her life, Mary was obedient to God's word and open to the power of the Holy Spirit at work in her. In this way, God's will was accomplished in and through her as a wife, mother, sister, friend, intercessor, and disciple of the Lord.

Mary shows us what God can realize in us: "God's love has been poured into our hearts through the Holy Spirit" (Romans 5:5). Through the Spirit, we are empowered to love and follow Jesus as his disciples today and to carry him in love to others.

Read and prayerfully reflect on these additional passages that describe the Holy Spirit and his power at work in humankind:

When thou sendest forth thy Spirit,
   they are created;
and thou renewest the face of the
   ground. (Psalm 104:30)

I will pour out my spirit upon all flesh; your sons and your daughters shall prophesy, your old men shall dream dreams, and your young men shall see visions. Even upon the menservants and maidservants in those days, I will pour out my spirit. (Joel 2:28-29)

You have received the spirit of sonship. When we cry "Abba! Father!" it is the Spirit himself bearing witness with our spirit that we are children of God, and if children, then heirs, heirs of God and fellow heirs with Christ. (Romans 8:15-17)

"What no eye has seen, nor ear heard, nor the heart of man conceived, what God has prepared for those who love him," God has revealed to us through the Spirit. For the Spirit searches everything, even the depths of God. For what person knows a man's thoughts except the spirit of the man which is in him? So also no one comprehends the thoughts of God except the Spirit of God. Now we have received not the spirit of the world, but the Spirit which is from God, that we might understand the gifts bestowed on us by God. (1 Corinthians 2:9-12)

In him you also, who have heard the word of truth, the gospel of your salvation, and have believed in him, were sealed with the promised Holy Spirit, who is the guarantee of our inheritance until we acquire possession of it, to the praise of his glory. (Ephesians 1:13-14)

Peter: Another Portrait of a Spirit-Filled Disciple

Read Acts 4:1-31

What a change the Holy Spirit made in the apostle Peter! After he received the Spirit on Pentecost, this man who had been so fearful that he denied his Lord and did not join the women in their vigil at Jesus' cross boldly preached the message of salvation to thousands (Acts 2:14-41). And when he was arrested by the Jewish authorities for healing a cripple in the name of Jesus Christ (Acts 3), Peter—"filled with the Holy Spirit" (4:8)—fearlessly declared, "There is salvation in no one else, for there is no other name under heaven given among men by which we must be saved. . . . We cannot but speak of what we have seen and heard" (4:12, 20).

These incidents are only the first among many recorded in the Acts of the Apostles about Peter after he was empowered by God's Spirit. Over and over again we read of the fruit borne and the lives transformed because of his obedience to the Spirit's direction. Peter's epistles to the young churches in Asia Minor also reflect the inspiration of the Spirit that was at work in him.

Like Mary, Peter was open to the Spirit even when he didn't understand: In one of the most important events in the spread of the Christian faith, Peter cooperated with God's surprising plan as the Spirit was poured out on Cornelius, who was a Gentile (Acts 10). Today countless men and women believe in Jesus as Lord and Messiah as a result of this apostle's trust in God and his openness to the Holy Spirit.

Treasuring the Word

A Reading from *Redemptoris Mater* by Pope John Paul II

The Mother of God at the Center of the Pilgrim Church

Built by Christ upon the Apostles, the Church became fully aware of these mighty works of God on the day of Pentecost, when those gathered together in the Upper Room "were all filled with the Holy Spirit and began to speak in other tongues, as the Spirit gave them utterance" (Acts 2:4). From that moment there also begins that journey of faith, the Church's pilgrimage through the history of individuals and peoples. We know that at the beginning of this journey Mary is present. We see her in the midst of the Apostles in the Upper Room, "prayerfully imploring the gift of the Spirit" (*Lumen Gentium*, 59).

In a sense her journey of faith is longer. The Holy Spirit had already come down upon her, and she became his faithful spouse at the Annunciation, welcoming the Word of the true God, offering "the full submission of intellect and will . . . and freely assenting to the truth revealed by him," indeed abandoning herself totally to God through "the obedience of faith," (*Dei Verbum*, 5) whereby she replied to the angel: "Behold, I am the handmaid of the Lord; let it be to me according to your word" (Luke 1:38). The journey of faith made by Mary, whom we see praying in the Upper Room, is thus longer than that of the others gathered there: Mary "goes before them," "leads the way" for them. (*LG*, 63) The moment of Pentecost in Jerusalem had been prepared for by the moment of the Annunciation in Nazareth, as well as by the Cross. In the Upper Room Mary's journey meets the Church's journey of faith. . . .

Above all, in the Church of that time and of every time Mary was and is the one who is "blessed because she believed" (Luke 1:45); she was the first to believe. From the moment of the Annunciation and conception, from the moment of his birth in the stable at Bethlehem, Mary followed Jesus step by step in her maternal pilgrimage of faith. She followed him during the years of his hidden life at Nazareth; she followed him also during the time after he left home, when he began "to do and to teach" (Acts 1:1) in the midst of Israel. Above all she followed him in the tragic experience of Golgotha. Now, while Mary was with the Apostles in the Upper Room in Jerusalem at the dawn of the Church, her faith, born from the words of the Annunciation, found confirmation. The angel had said to her then: "You will conceive in your womb and bear a son, and you shall call his name

Jesus. He will be great . . . and he will reign over the house of Jacob for ever; and of his kingdom there will be no end" (Luke 1:31-33). The recent events on Calvary had shrouded that promise in darkness, yet not even beneath the Cross did Mary's faith fail. She had still remained the one who, like Abraham, "in hope believed against hope" (Romans 4:18). But it is only after the Resurrection that hope had shown its true face and the promise had begun to be transformed into reality. For Jesus, before returning to the Father, had said to the Apostles: "Go therefore and make disciples of all nations . . . lo, I am with you always, to the close of the age" (Matthew 28:19-20). Thus had spoken the one who by his Resurrection had revealed himself as the conqueror of death, as the one who possessed the kingdom of which, as the angel said, "there will be no end."

Now, at the first dawn of the Church, at the beginning of the long journey through faith which began at Pentecost in Jerusalem, Mary was with all those who were the seed of the "new Israel." She was present among them as an exceptional witness to the mystery of Christ. And the Church was assiduous in prayer together with her, and at the same time "contemplated her in the light of the Word made man." It was always to be so. For when the Church "enters more intimately into the supreme mystery of the Incarnation," she thinks of the Mother of Christ with profound reverence and devotion. (*LG*, 65) Mary belongs indissolubly to the mystery of Christ, and she belongs also to the mystery of the Church from the beginning, from the day of the Church's birth. At the basis of what the Church has been from the beginning, and of what she must continually become from generation to generation, in the midst of all the nations of the earth, we find the one "who believed that there would be a fulfillment of what was spoken to her from the Lord" (Luke 1:45). It is precisely Mary's faith which marks the beginning of the new and eternal Covenant of God with man in Jesus Christ; this heroic faith of hers "precedes" the apostolic witness of the Church, and ever remains in the Church's heart hidden like a special heritage of God's revelation. All those who from generation to generation accept the apostolic witness of the Church share in that mysterious inheritance, and in a sense share in Mary's faith. (26, 27)

Source Notes and Acknowledgments

This section indicates the sources of material quoted in *My Soul Magnifies the Lord: A Scriptural Journey with Mary*.

Introduction

Page 5:
John Paul II, *Theotókos Woman, Mother, Disciple: A Catechesis on Mary, Mother of God* (Boston: Pauline Books & Media, 2000), p. 199.

Catechism of the Catholic Church (San Francisco: Ignatius Press), 466, p. 117; 499, p. 126; 491, pp. 122-123; 966, p. 252.

Reflection 1: The Annunciation

Page 8:
Mother Teresa, *Jesus, the Word to Be Spoken*, compiled by Brother Angelo Devananda (Ann Arbor, Mich.: Servant Books, 1986), p. 47.

Page 13:
Bernard of Clairvaux, *Homilies in Praise of the Blessed Virgin Mary*, trans. Marie-Bernard Saïd (Kalamazoo, Mich.: Cistercian Publications, 1993), p. 54.

John Paul II, *Tertio Millennio Adveniente* (Apostolic Letter "On Preparation for the Jubilee of the Year 2000"), 48. Promulgated on 10 November 1994. Available at the Web site www.vatican.va

Page 20:
Augustine: Quoted in John Saward, *Redeemer in the Womb: Jesus Living in Mary* (San Francisco: Ignatius Press, 1993), pp. 104-105.

Pages 22-23:
Caryll Houselander, *The Reed of God* (Allen, Tex.: Christian Classics, Inc., 1996), pp. 11-13. Copyright © 1944 by Caryll Houselander.

Reflection 2: The Visitation

Page 24:
Adrienne von Speyr, *Handmaid of the Lord*, trans. E. A. Nelson (San Francisco: Ignatius Press, 1985), p. 52.

Page 27:
Cardinal Pierre de Bérulle: Quoted in Saward, pp. 91-92.

Page 28:
Bede the Venerable: Quoted in *The Liturgy of the Hours, Volume II* (New York: Catholic Book Publishing Co., 1976), pp.1846-1847.

Pages 37-38:
John Paul II, *Theotókos Woman, Mother, Disciple*, pp. 139-141.

Reflection 3: The Nativity

Page 40:
Augustine: Quoted in Raniero Cantalamessa, *Mary, Mirror of the Church*, trans. Frances Lonergan Villa (Collegeville, Minn.: The Liturgical Press, 1972), p. 74.

Page 45:
Romano Guardini, *The Lord*, trans. Elinor Castendyk Briefs (Washington, D.C.: Regnery Publishing, Inc., 1996), pp. 16, 17.

Page 53:
John Paul II, *Rosarium Virginis Mariae* (Apostolic Letter "On the Most Holy Rosary"), 10. Promulgated on 16 October 2002. Available at the Web site www.vatican.va

Page 54:
Irenaeus and *Jerome*. Quoted in *Lumen Gentium* (Dogmatic Constitution of the Church), 56. Issued on 24 November 1964. Available at the Web site www.vatican.va

Pages 55-56:
Raniero Cantalamessa, *Mary, Mirror of the Church*, trans. Frances Lonergan Villa (Collegeville, Minn.: The Liturgical Press, 1972), pp. 56-57. Copyright © 1972 by The Order of St. Benedict, Inc. Reprinted with permission.

Reflection 4: The Presentation

Page 58:
Sophronius: Quoted in *The Liturgy of the Hours, Volume III* (New York: Catholic Book Publishing Co., 1975), p. 1350.

Page 62:
John Paul II, *Redemptoris Mater* (Encyclical Letter "Mother of the Redeemer"), 16. Promulgated on 25 March 1987. Available at the Web site www.vatican.va

Pages 71-72:
Edward Leen, C.S. Sp., "The Presentation in the Temple," from *The Mary Book*, assembled by F.J. Sheed (New York: Sheed & Ward, 1951), pp. 122-125. Copyright © 1950 by Sheed & Ward, Inc. This material originally appeared in *In the Likeness of Christ* by Edward Leen (New York: Sheed & Ward, 1936). Reprinted with permission of Sheed & Ward, an imprint of the Rowman & Littlefield Publishing Group, Inc., Lanham, Maryland.

Reflection 5: The Adoration of the Magi

Page 74:
Peter Chrysologus: Quoted in *The Liturgy of the Hours, Volume I* (New York: Catholic Book Publishing Co., 1975), p. 578.

Page 79:
Sister Wendy Beckett, *Sister Wendy's Nativity* (Chicago: Loyola Press, 1998), p. 48.

Page 87:
John Paul II, *Rosarium Virginis Mariae*, 10.

Pages 89-90:
Saint Bernard on the Christian Year: Selections from His Sermons, trans. A Religious of C.S.M.V. (London: A.R. Mowbray, 1954), pp. 48-49, 54.

Reflection 6: The Flight into Egypt

Page 92:
Alfred Delp, S.J., *The Prison Meditations of Father Alfred Delp* (New York: Herder and Herder, 1963), pp. 80-81.

Page 98:
F.J. Sheed, *To Know Christ Jesus* (San Francisco: Ignatius Press, 1992), p. 61.

John Paul II, *Redemptoris Mater*, 17.

Page 106:
Paul VI, *Marialis Cultus* (Apostolic Exhortation "For the Right Ordering and Development of Devotion to the Blessed Virgin Mary"), 37. Promulgated 2 February 1974. Available at the Web site www.vatican.va

Pages 108-109:
Ignacio Larrañaga, O.F.M. Cap., *The Silence of Mary*, trans. V. Gaudet, O.M.I. (Boston: Pauline Books & Media), pp. 87-90. English edition copyright © 1991 by Daughters of St. Paul. Original Title: *El silencio de María*. Copyright © 1979, Cefepal, Santiago de Chile. Reprinted with permission of the Capuchinos de Chile.

Reflection 7: The Finding of the Child Jesus in the Temple

Page 110:
Fulton J. Sheen, *The World's First Love* (San Francisco: Ignatius Press, 1996), p. 218.

Page 115:
Bernard of Clairvaux: Quoted in Francis Fernandez, *In Conversation with God – Volume Six*, (London: Scepter Ltd., 1997), pp. 3-4.

Augustine: Quoted in Francis Fernandez, *In Conversation with God – Volume One*, (London: Scepter Ltd., 1988), p. 361.

John Paul II, *Redemptoris Mater*, 17.

Page 122:
St. Alphonsus de Liguori, *The Glories of Mary* (Brooklyn, N.Y.: Redemptorist Fathers), Fourth Reprint Revised, p. 509.

Origen: Quoted in St. Alphonsus de Liguori, p. 509.

Page 123:
Blaise Arminjon, S.J., *The Cantata of Love*, trans, Nelly Marans (San Francisco: Ignatius Press), p. 187.

Pages 124-125:
Houselander, pp. 91-93.

Reflection 8: The Wedding at Cana

Page 126:
Paul VI, *Marialis Cultus*, 18.

Page 130:
Sheen, pp. 112-113.

Catechism of the Catholic Church, 1613, p. 403.

John Paul II, *Theotókos Woman, Mother, Disciple*, p. 174.

Page 131:
Ibid., p. 175.

Page 138:
Alphonsus Liguori: Quoted in *The Navarre Bible: The Gospel of St. John,* with a commentary by the members of the Faculty of Theology of the University of Navarre (Blackrock, Ireland: Four Courts Press, 1995), p. 63.

Sub tuum praesidium: Quoted in Anthony F. Chiffolo, *100 Names of Mary: Stories & Prayers* (Cincinnati: St. Anthony Messenger Press, 2002), p. 2.

Pages 140-141:
Fulton J. Sheen, *The World's First Love* (San Francisco: Ignatius Press, 1996), pp. 163-164. Reprinted with permission of Ignatius Press, San Francisco, CA.

Reflection 9: At the Foot of the Cross

Page 142:
John Paul II: Quoted in *The Navarre Bible: The Gospel of St. John,* p. 232.

Page 146:
John Paul II, *Theotókos Woman, Mother, Disciple,* pp. 188-189

Page 147:
Thomas of Jesus: Quoted in *Mary's Yes: Meditations on Mary through the Ages,* ed. John E. Rotelle, O.S.A. (Ann Arbor, Mich.: Servant Publications, 1989), p. 109

Sheen, p. 259.

Pages 156-157:
Romanos the Melodist, "Mary at the Cross," from *The Penguin Book of Greek Verse,* trans. Constantine Trypanis (Middlesex, England: Penguin Books Ltd., 1971), pp. 404-405, 410, 411-414. Reprinted with permission of Penguin Books Ltd.

Reflection 10: Pentecost

Page 158:
John Paul II, *Rosarium Virginis Mariae,* 23.

Page 162:
Carlo Martini, *Our Lady of Holy Saturday* (Liguori, Mo.: Liguori Publications, 2002), p. 29.

Joseph Ratzinger, "The Sign of the Woman: An Introduction to the Encyclical *Redemptoris Mater*" from *Mary: God's Yes to Man* (San Francisco: Ignatius Press, 1988), p. 35.

Page 163:
John Paul II, *Theotókos Woman, Mother, Disciple,* p. 198-199.

Ibid., p. 199.

Page 164:
Catechism of the Catholic Church, 966, p. 252.

Pages 173-174:
John Paul II, *Redemptoris Mater,* 26, 27.

Marian Resources

In addition to the resources listed in the Source Notes and Acknowledgments, the following may be of interest to readers who would like more information on Mary:

The Mary Page Web site: www.udayton.edu/mary/main.html

The Mary Page is maintained by The Marian Library/International Marian Research Institute, an international center of research and study on the role of Mary in Christian life. The Institute is located at the University of Dayton in Ohio.

Notes

Notes

Notes

Notes

Notes

Notes

Also in the Scriptural Journey Series

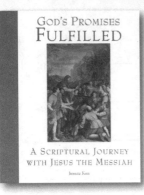

God's Promises Fulfilled:
A Scriptural Journey with Jesus the Messiah
by Jeanne Kun

Each of the ten reflections on key biblical passages will help you come to know Jesus in his role as Messiah, the Savior of the world. The first three chapters focus on Old Testament passages that unfold the promises of God, while the remaining chapters present gospel scenes that portray Jesus as the fulfillment of those promises. Suitable for group or individual use.
192 pages, 7⅜ x 9, softcover, $12.95 Item# BIGJE6

"God's Promises Fulfilled: A Scriptural Journey with Jesus the Messiah is more than a mere 'Bible study.' Studying the Bible engages our wits. Pondering the Bible puts us in the same school as the Blessed Virgin herself, who 'pondered these things in her heart' and who thereby constantly grew in holiness and love. I highly recommend this book as a way to ponder the words of Scripture."
> Mark P. Shea, senior content editor
> CatholicExchange.com

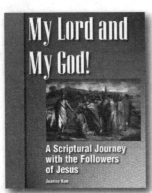

My Lord and My God!
A Scriptural Journey with the Followers of Jesus
by Jeanne Kun

Jesus deeply touched the lives of those who became his disciples, followers, and friends. *My Lord and My God! A Scriptural Journey with the Followers of Jesus* is based on ten gospel characters who encountered Jesus in a life-changing way. Simon Peter, Bartimaeus, Mary of Bethany, Joseph of Arimathea, Thomas—and others—show just how diverse the faces of discipleship are. This book is suitable for small-group discussion or individual use. 192 pages, 7⅜ x 9, softcover, $12.95 Item# BDSCE5

"Once again I'm inspired by a work from Jeanne Kun. She has a gift, born from her own experience of the ways of God, to assist us in encountering Christ. In her latest book, *My Lord and My God! A Scriptural Journey with the Followers of Jesus,* biblical figures come to life, and we meet the Lord Jesus Christ with them."
> Fr. Jeffrey Huard, director of campus ministry
> University of St. Thomas
> St. Paul, Minnesota